LIFE AFTER DEATH IN WORLD RELIGIONS

FAITH MEETS FAITH

An Orbis Series in Interreligious Dialogue
Paul F. Knitter, General Editor

In the contemporary world, the many religions and spiritualities stand in need of greater communication and cooperation. More than ever before, they must speak to, learn from, and work with each other in order both to maintain their vital identities and to contribute to fashioning a better world.

FAITH MEETS FAITH seeks to promote interreligious dialogue by providing an open forum for exchanges among followers of different religious paths. While the Series wants to encourage creative and bold responses to questions arising from contemporary appreciations of religious plurality, it also recognizes the multiplicity of basic perspectives concerning the methods and content of interreligious dialogue.

Although rooted in a Christian theological perspective, the Series does not endorse any single school of thought or approach. By making available to both the scholarly community and the general public works that represent a variety of religious and methodological viewpoints, FAITH MEETS FAITH seeks to foster an encounter among followers of the religions of the world on matters of common concern.

Faith Meets Faith Series

LIFE AFTER DEATH IN WORLD RELIGIONS

edited by

Harold Coward

ORBIS BOOKS

Maryknoll, New York 10545

Fourth Printing,April 2000

Published by Orbis Books, Maryknoll, New York, U.S.A.

Manufactured in the United States of America.
Manuscript editing and typesetting by Joan Marie Laflamme

Library of Congress Cataloging in Publication Data

Life after death in world religions / edited by Harold Coward.
p. cm. — (Faith meets faith series)
Includes bibliographical references and index.
ISBN 1-57075-119-6 (alk. paper)
1. Future life—Comparative studies. 2. Death—Religious aspects—Comparative studies. I. Coward, Harold G. II. Series: Faith meets faith.
BL535.L544 1997
291.2'3—dc21 96-51083
CIP

Contents

Preface

The chapters in this book evolved from lectures given in the annual Distinguished Speakers Series organized by the Centre for Studies in Religion and Society and co-sponsored by the University of Victoria's Division of Continuing Studies.

The Centre for Studies in Religion and Society was established at the University of Victoria in 1991 to foster the scholarly study of religion in relation to the sciences, ethics, social and economic development, and other aspects of culture. The primary aim is to promote dialogue between religion and these other aspects of human experience. The Centre has a fundamental commitment to pluralism and pursues a broad range of research interests not limited to any specific time, place, religion, or culture. It embodies the understanding that religious traditions have been formative of human reality and experience, and that the speeches are the proper object of creative, rigorous inquiry, whether from a disciplinary or an interdisciplinary perspective.

Each year the Centre invites distinguished scholars from various religions to speak on a common theme from the perspective of their own traditions. The 1995 Distinguished Speakers Series on Life After Death evoked such strong and positive audience response that the speeches were augmented and revised for publication as a book.

Thanks are due to the Centre's Administrator, Ludgard De Decker, for her careful preparation of the manuscript and to Cora Smith for the index. As always, it has been a pleasure to work with William Burrows and his staff at Orbis Books in the publishing of this volume.

Harold Coward
Director
Centre for Studies in Religion and Society
University of Victoria
Victoria, British Columbia, Canada

Introduction

Is there life after death? This is one of the fundamental questions that none of us escapes. As we grow old or suffer the loss of a loved one, this question commands our attention. Although much in life has changed over the centuries, when it comes to death and what happens after, we are little different than our ancestors. Although modern medicine keeps many of us alive longer, death inevitably holds sway. Then, like previous generations, we find ourselves face to face with that which we cannot scientifically control or understand.

The theologian Paul Tillich said that theology is correlational—that theology begins with the questions life asks and then searches scripture and tradition for answers.[1] The vitality of any religion is indicated by its ability to provide satisfying answers to our deepest and most difficult questions.

Throughout history the great religions have provided answers to the question, Is there life after death, and, if so, what is it like? The religions also have offered rituals to help embody these answers in daily life.

With separate chapters for Judaism, Christianity, Islam, Hinduism, Buddhism, and the Chinese religions, this book allows the reader to examine the differences and similarities in the way that these religions respond to the question, Is there life after death? Each chapter begins by briefly sketching the basic beliefs of that religion before focusing on its views of death and life after death. This enables readers with no previous background in the religion to understand the answer to the question in the larger context of that tradition. The chapters also include discussion of different answers offered within each religion and critical problems that may remain unresolved. Each religion is presented by a leading scholar of that tradition. The authors have endeavored to write in ways that do not oversimplify the difficult concepts involved and yet make them accessible to the beginning student of religion or the serious lay reader.

Within each of these religions there are many different doctrines and rituals relating to life after death. A comprehensive treatment would require a separate book for each religion. Without attempting to be exhaustive, each author presents a balanced overview of the answer to the question, Is there life after death? There are many religions not included (e.g., Sikhism, Jainism, Shintoism, and the Aboriginal traditions), all of which have important ideas and rituals relating to life after death. In a small introductory book one has to make choices, and in this case it was decided to focus on the larger world religions. A future volume is planned in which the traditions omitted in this volume will be highlighted.

THE WESTERN RELIGIONS—JUDAISM, CHRISTIANITY, AND ISLAM

Judaism's approach to life after death is foundational for Christianity and Islam as well. Judaism is unique among religions in starting from the viewpoint that there is no survival after death—immortality is only through one's children, as Segal makes clear in his chapter. Later the idea of a bodily resurrection becomes common, although rejected by one Jewish sect, the Sadducees. After the fall of the Temple in Jerusalem (ca. 70 C.E.) the Rabbinic view develops the notion that the dead will be restored to their own bodies in a future age under the leadership of the Messiah. Some thought the wicked would be punished in their graves while waiting for the coming of the Messiah. Thus the idea that while waiting for the Messiah the righteous would go to a heavenly paradise while the sinners experience Gehenna or hell developed. The Jewish mystics, the Kabbalists, formulated the idea that one aspect of the soul returns at death to God, its source.

Christianity takes over most of these basic ideas but adds additional qualifications. Salvation, in terms of resurrection from the dead, is made possible for Christians by Jesus' own resurrection. Thus the importance of the post-resurrection appearances where Jesus met his followers, demonstrating the fact that he was raised from the dead and that, if faithful, they too would be raised. In the Christian view, without Christ's resurrection all would be doomed to eternal death. Christ's victory over death, however, makes possible eternal life for all. As Paul puts it in 1 Corinthians 15:22-23: "As in Adam all men die, so in Christ all will be brought to life; but each in his own proper place: Christ the firstfruits, and afterwards, at his coming, those who belong to Christ." Paul also discusses the nature of the resurrected body, saying that the animal body that has died will be succeeded by a spiritual body. Penelhum, in his chapter on Christianity, provides a clear and careful analysis of Christian attempts to understand the nature of the post-resurrection spiritual body. Against tendencies of some present-day Christians to emphasize the Kingdom of God in this life to the exclusion of the afterlife, Penelhum makes clear that it is essential for Christians to believe that there is an afterlife and that its nature is that of an individual bodily resurrection—albeit a spiritual body.

Kassis sets forth the Islamic conception of the afterlife over and against the pre-Islamic tribal views of the Arabian Peninsula. In the pre-Islamic view, death came as a result of the cessation of either breath or blood. Natural death resulted from the cessation of breath. By contrast, death from the shedding of blood was considered unnatural and required retribution without which the soul of the dead wandered the desert restlessly until avenged—the duty of the tribe to which the dead person belonged. Islam radically changed these conceptions. The tribe was replaced by the *ummah*, the universal community of faith. Each individual belonged to God, not to the tribe. Like Judaism and Christianity, Islam teaches that it is God who gives life and takes it away. For the pre-Islamic Arabs, death was a realm of torpor into which one passed at the end of life on earth. Islam, however, saw death not as the end of life but as a passageway from perishable earthly life to the permanence of eternal life in the hereafter, with God ruling both. For Muslims, judgment begins in the tomb soon after death when the deceased is visited by two angels and made to sit up in the grave and answer questions of faith. Correct responses meant that one was left to rest in peace until Jesus the Messiah and Satan the anti-Christ return to do battle on the Day of Resurrection of the dead. Here Islam borrows many ideas from its sister religions of Christianity and Judaism. No one but God knows when that hour or day will be. It will be announced by terrible portents such as earthquakes, fire, and the failure of the sun to rise. Satan, because of his resemblance to Christ, will at first entice many Muslims to follow him. But then Jesus, the Messiah, will appear to do battle and defeat Satan, restoring the reign of faith, justice, and peace until the Day of Judgment. According to the Qur'ān, on that day, at the sound of the trumpet, all the dead will return to life and individually come to stand before God to read the record of their own actions and be judged. The righteous will be admitted to Paradise, while the wicked will suffer a second punishment by being sent to dwell in the fires of Hell (Gehenna) forever.

THE EASTERN RELIGIONS—HINDUISM, BUDDHISM, AND THE CHINESE TRADITIONS

Turning to the Eastern Religions we find very different ideas about death and life after death. Fundamental to the Hindu world view is the notion that each person is being continually reborn—life after life after life. A second basic idea is that this rebirth continuum has been going on without beginning. What a person does or thinks in each life conditions the circumstances and predispositions (*karma*) that will be experienced in future lives. And the dispositions one experiences in this life are the result of one's actions in past lives. This basic Hindu idea of birth-death-rebirth (*karma-saṃsāra*) was adopted by Buddhism, Jainism, and Sikhism.

While this way of thinking seems strange and foreign to our Western minds, it is supported by a well-worked-out theory that follows with clear logic once its basic assumptions are granted. These assumptions involve the notions of rebirth and the law of karma. The law of karma maintains that every time we do an action or think a thought, a memory trace is laid down in the unconscious. A good action or thought leaves behind its trace, as does an evil action or thought.[2] When we find ourselves in a similar situation in the future, the previous memory trace rises up in consciousness as an impulse to do a similar action or think a similar thought. Note that this is merely an *impulse* (a disposition or desire) and in itself does not force us to repeat the good or evil action or thought. We still have free choice. We may decide to go with the impulse and repeat the action (in which case a reinforced memory trace will be laid down in the unconscious) or to negate the impulse (in which case, using the analogy of the seed, the sprouting impulse will receive neither warmth nor nourishment and will wither away leaving no further trace in the unconscious). Thus by the exercise of free choice at each moment in life we either reinforce or delete the memory traces in our unconscious. In theory, then, every impulse we experience in this life should be traceable to actions or thoughts done since birth. But karma theory does not assume a *tabula rasa* or blank mind at birth. Not only does our unconscious contain memory traces of all actions and thoughts since birth but also those from the life before this, and the life before that, and so on backward infinitely (karma theory rejects any absolute beginning and assumes that life has always been going on). Consequently each of us is thought to have in our unconscious a huge store of memory traces that is constantly bursting with ideas, impulses, desires to this or that good or bad action or thought. These impulses, however, can be controlled by the exercise of free choice. If a particular action or thought is repeated often enough it becomes a habit. The result of this theory is a ladder of existence as follows:

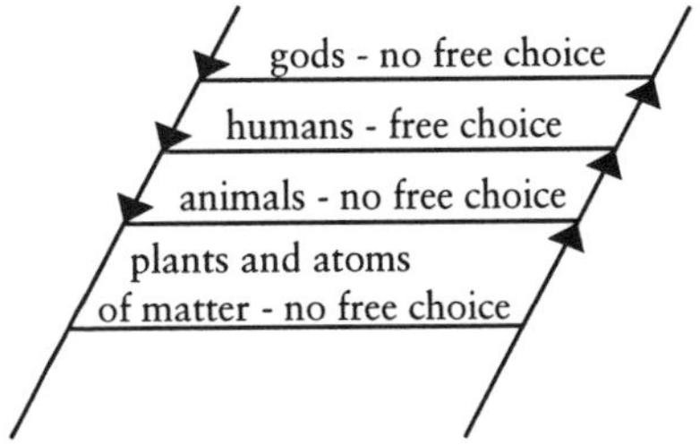

Figure 1: The Karmic Ladder of Existence

Assume that you are a human being. If you use your free choice to act on the good karmic impulses that come up within consciousness and negate the evil impulses, then at the end of this life you will have increased the number of good karmas (memory traces) in your unconscious and reduced the number of evil karmas. Using the image of a banker's balance, this will automatically cause you to be reborn higher up the scale. If in your next and future lives you continue to act on the good and negate the evil, you will spiral up the ladder of existence until you are eventually reborn as a god. Gods are beings just like us who, according to mythology, have the honor of superintending one of the cosmic functions (e.g., the sun god). But this is merely an honor and carries no free choice. Once the merit from all the good free choices you made as a human is used up, you are reborn as a human being once again with free choice.

But now let us follow through the other possibility, namely, that in this life you use your free choice to reinforce the evil impulses and negate the good. At death you will have increased the number of evil impulses and reduced the number of good impulses. This will automatically cause you to be born a step lower on the ladder of existence. If the same pattern is repeated in the next life and the next and so on, you will spiral downward until eventually you are reborn as an animal. Animals are beings like you and me but with a heavier composition of evil karmas (memory traces). Animals have no free choice but simply endure the sufferings to which their animal instincts expose them. Through these sufferings the evil karmas built up from years of evil choices (made freely as human beings) are expiated. Then you are reborn as a human again with free choice and the ability to move up or down the ladder through karma and rebirth. In the Jaina view, plants and atoms of matter are treated as parallel to animals.

This is indeed a "long view" on life after death. After countless lifetimes it might well lead one to voice the sentiment "Stop the world, I want to get off!"—or in Eastern terms, "Is there not some way out of this beginningless and seemingly endless cycle of birth, death, and rebirth?" The Hindu religion gives one answer (one path out of this revolving afterlife), the Buddhist religion another, and the Jainas a third—all quite different. In this book we restrict ourselves to a detailed examination of the Hindu and Buddhist answers leaving the Jaina answer to a later volume.

In detailing the Hindu answer Rambachan describes exactly how the self is reborn in a series of bodies, life after life. What carries the karmic memory traces from one life to the next is not the self or soul but the subtle body (*sūkṣma śarīra*), which separates from the physical body at death. Changing physical bodies at death, says Hindu scripture, is like changing worn-out clothes. But how does one escape the treadmill of endless rebirths? Rambachan outlines the two main possibilities provided for in the Hindu answer: (a) be reborn in heaven (*svarga*) with the gods and enjoy a temporary respite until one's accumulated spiritual merit is used up, at which time one is reborn again in the human realm; or (b) under the guidance of a teacher pursue the spiritual discipline taught in the Upaniṣads (knowledge and meditation) until one realizes the identity of one's self with God (Brahman), the essence of all things, and is released from further rebirth (*mokṣa*).

In her description of the Buddhist answer, Neumaier-Dargyay begins with the basic challenge to Buddhist teaching; namely, if, as the Buddha taught, there is no self, then what is reborn? After reviewing the answers of the Pali or Theravada tradition, she offers a detailed presentation of the Mahayana Tibetan Buddhist perspective as found in the *Tibetan Book of the Dead* (the *Bar do thos grol*) or more accurately, *The Tibetan Book of "Liberation from the Intermediary State by Means of Hearing This Lore."* This text tells how, at the moment of death, one who is sufficiently advanced in spiritual discipline will see the luminosity of the Buddha Nature and recognize it as being indistinguishable from one's own mind in its pure form. Such a person realizes enlightenment or *nirvana*. People of lesser spiritual attainment will also see the luminosity but only for the flash of a second and may feel frightened by it. They are not yet at the level of karmic purity required for enlightenment and so will be reborn with an opportunity for further spiritual development. Such a person, at death, is described by the text as being in an intermediate state for a period of time while searching for a new physical body (a fetus) in which it can be reborn. The text suggests that careful study of it during one's life and a clear remembering of it at the moment of death can enable one to avoid rebirth by realizing nirvana or enlightenment.

Neumaier-Dargyay notes that this sophisticated Buddhist analysis of death, rebirth, and enlightenment may connect with recent reports of near-death experiences in which some primary transcultural phenomena seem to be present, that is, the perception of brilliant light, the "seeing" of one's old body, the feeling of not being confined by one's physical body yet having sensations of it, and finally, the "observation" of relatives and friends in their experiences of death.

Arbuckle, in his chapter on life after death in Chinese religions, conveys a sense of how the Buddhist ideas of India blended with the Confucian and Daoist ideas native to China. Religion in China has the reputation of being pragmatic in its motivation. He shows how the notion of a heavenly bureaucracy produced by Confucian thinkers is able to keep up to date even to the point of positing money and credit cards written on the Bank of Hell.

Chinese religious thought and practice has been likened to a stew-pot in which any one ingredient (*te*) is blended with all of the others in order to express most fully its own flavor.[3] Arbuckle shows how Confucian, Buddhist, and Daoist ideas of the afterworld and its interaction with this world are blended in a rich and imaginative yet sustaining stew for those living. The chapter recounts Chinese thinking on the "cosmos and the theory of the soul," "going to one's reward," "prison breaks: philosophy, alchemy, escape, endurance," and "the afterlife in modern times."

Arbuckle concludes that the rich mix of Chinese ideas regarding death and the afterlife is alive and well in contemporary Chinese culture, especially in places like Taiwan, Hong Kong, and Vancouver. Even in Mainland China, he maintains, the country people who make up the vast majority of China's population never forgot their gods or their requirements for life now and in the hereafter.

These chapters present the age-old wisdom of six world religions on the fundamental question, Is there life after death, and, if so, what is it like—and how does it affect me while I am alive? Although our modern world has focused on the pleasures and sorrows of this life, there comes a time when each of us is faced with the prospect of our own death or shaken by the death of a loved one. At such moments worldly pleasures, material securities, and scientific certainties fade, to be replaced by the age old questions about death and life after death. To such questions the wisdom of the religions—wisdom that has stood the test of satisfying countless generations—offers important answers worthy of careful consideration.

Notes

[1] Paul Tillich, *Systematic Theology*, vol. 1 (Chicago: University of Chicago Press, 1951), p. 61.

[2] The criteria for good or evil are determined as follows: For a Hindu, good and evil actions or thoughts are defined in the revealed scripture, the Veda. In Buddhism, where there is no God or revealed scripture, good or evil is defined in terms of the intention motivating the action or thought (e.g., the intention to harm one's neighbor, dog, or field produces an evil karma or memory trace). For a philosophical study of karma see B. R. Reichenbach, *The Law of Karma: A Philosophical Study* (Honolulu: University of Hawaii Press, 1990).

[3] R. T. Ames, "Putting the *Te* back into Taoism," in *Nature in Asian Traditions of Thought: Essays in Environmental Philosophy*, ed. J. B. Callicott and R. T. Ames (Albany: State University of New York Press, 1989), p. 126.

1

Judaism

Eliezer Segal

The term *Judaism*, which implies a definable belief-system, has no real equivalent in the traditional vocabulary of the religion itself. Its widespread use in European languages owes largely to the encounter with Christianity, which attaches greater importance to creeds and doctrines. In Jewish tradition, theology and religious concepts rarely have been perceived as defining features.

It is more accurate to employ the term *Judaism* in a broader cultural sense to denote the full range of religious expressions of the people of Israel (as they almost invariably have referred to themselves). This usage correctly underscores the national character of the religion, inextricably bound to historical experience, without attaching disproportionate weight to its theological component. As we shall observe, Judaism contains a complex variety of elements, including law, ethics, morality, observances, worship, and beliefs.

Technically, the word *Judaism*—like its cognate terms *Jew* and *Jewish*—refers to a more narrowly defined time frame within the longer national history, commencing at the conclusion of the biblical era. Whereas earlier epochs had known of twelve tribes of Israel, or of the two rival monarchies of Judah and Israel, a sequence of conquests and exiles brought about a situation in which only a vestige of the original people, dominated by the ancient tribe of Judah and inhabiting its ancestral territory (Judea), was able to maintain its religious and cultural identity through subsequent generations. In some recent scholarship and theological writing it has become common to restrict the use of *Judaism* to those manifestations that emerged after the Babylonian exile, as distinct from earlier *Israelite* or *Hebrew* religion. We must take care not to construe this terminological preference as an assertion that the Judaism of the Second Temple era (see below) was a new and original invention, unconnected to the religion of the Hebrew scriptures.

If indeed there is a term from Judaism's own conceptual vocabulary that can serve as a meaningful alternative to *Judaism*, it is undoubtedly *Torah*. From its basic connotations of "teaching" or "guidance," Torah came to be equated with the scriptures that were revealed by God to Israel through the agency of Moses, the greatest of God's messengers or *prophets*. The text of this revelation was written down in the volumes that Jews refer to as the Torah, usually designated in English as "the Five Books of Moses" (reflecting the old Greek term *Pentateuch*). Although the Torah consists largely of laws and observances, it contains other elements, particularly a historical narrative. The Torah of Moses is the most sacred and authoritative component of the Jewish scriptures, which also include two other sections: the "Prophets" [Hebrew: *Nevi'im*] and the "[Sacred] Writings" [Hebrew: *Ketuvim*; Greek: *Hagiographa*]. Taken together, the Jewish scriptures are usually referred to as the Hebrew Bible; Christians designate them the Old Testament (OT).

According to the view that would eventually become normative in Judaism, the five books of the Written Torah were paralleled by an oral revelation that is an equally authentic and holy part of the divine revelation to Moses. Though the earliest mentions of the Oral Torah referred to venerable ancestral traditions that had been transmitted over the generations, the concept of Oral Torah evolved to encompass additional aspects of religious lore, including the enactments and teachings ascribed to the sages of various generations, interpretations of biblical precepts, and so forth. Thus, in its broader and dynamic meaning, the word

Torah can refer to the rich spectrum of Jewish religious traditions as they evolved through the ages. The delicate interplay of Oral and Written Torahs will be very much in evidence when we attempt to trace the evolution of Jewish conceptions of the afterlife.

Judaism's characteristic subordination of creed to practice allowed for a surprising range of theological expression over the ages, frequently in response to foreign stimuli. In keeping with the evolving, historical character of Jewish religion, we shall divide our treatment of the topic into several chronological stages.

THE FIRST COMMONWEALTH (until ca. 539 B.C.E.)[1]

The authors of the Hebrew Bible, apart from its latest strata, did not teach that individuals survive death in any religiously significant way. Although there are several terms and passages in the Hebrew scriptures that could allude to some sort of afterlife conception, and others that would be creatively interpreted in that vein by Jews of later generations, their place in the broader context of biblical world views is negligible.

Take, for example, the words of those classical prophets who devoted their lives to instilling in their contemporaries a zeal for God and the Torah. If they had anticipated that the dead would be judged in a future world, or that their spiritual immortality was contingent upon their religious and moral conduct in their present lives, then it is inconceivable why this argument is absent from their impassioned preaching. Neither is one's destiny in the afterlife cited as a reason for sacrificial atonement or to explain the necessity for cleansing oneself of sins and impurities. Several passages in the Torah present ghastly lists of curses that will befall the Israelites should they fail to hearken unto God's word. Among these stark descriptions of the consequences of disobedience, we read about plagues and fevers, defeat and conquest, famine, desolation, and exile. Yet nowhere do we encounter any mention of the fate that awaits the sinners upon conclusion of their days on earth. Even when the Torah is emphasizing that God's grace or wrath will continue beyond a person's life span, it does so by extending it to one's progeny. For better or for worse, it was believed that immortality would be achieved through the continuity of future generations rather than in a supernatural afterlife.

Alongside these eloquent arguments from silence, we must acknowledge that there are texts in the Hebrew Bible that give a different impression, that seem to refer to at least a limited kind of afterlife. In the following pages we shall survey some of the principal pieces of evidence that have been adduced by scholars.

The Bible frequently speaks of deceased persons being "gathered unto their fathers" or "sleeping with their fathers." The expressions evoke a picture of the dead ancestors existing in some state, awaiting reunification with their recently deceased descendants. However, they could mean no more than "they followed their forefathers into death and the grave."

Another common biblical expression for death is to "go down to *she'ol*." It has become almost universal to render the term as "the underworld," or even as "hell," and to describe it as a shadowy place of disembodied spirits, similar to the Greek conception of Hades.

When we examine the actual passages in which the word *she'ol* appears, we find few, if any, that cannot plausibly be understood simply as "pit" or (by extension) "grave," which became a figurative equivalent for death. In some passages *she'ol* refers to underground realms that have no associations with death. Even those texts that present *she'ol* as a frightening fate in store for the wicked do not necessarily imply more than that the sinners will bring upon themselves an early death.[2] Early scholarly attempts to identify an etymological link with an Assyrian term for the abode of dead spirits have proven to be spurious, based on preconceived ideas and extratextual considerations.[3]

The most compelling proof for biblical belief in survival after death is the disturbing tale, related in 1 Samuel 28, of how the desperate King Saul clandestinely visited the "witch of Endor," who called up the departed spirit of the prophet Samuel. If we accept the story at face value, then the ghostly spirit of the prophet

Samuel lingered on in a restful state until his repose was disturbed by the terrified Israelite monarch. It is not entirely clear from the narrative whether Samuel was aware of the events that had been troubling Saul or if he was merely drawing conclusions based on the information supplied by Saul and his own memory of God's hostility toward the king.

Several details raise doubts about the narrator's perspective on the episode. The fact that Saul himself did not behold the prophet but relied on the witch's description suggests that she might have staged a hoax for his benefit, although the wording implies that it was Samuel who spoke the words that Saul heard. Some have preferred to construe the whole apparition as a vision manufactured by God for the occasion. Nevertheless, it is probable that the story's author truly believed that deceased souls linger on in a state of repose, subject to disturbances by necromancers and other mortal nuisances.

Even if the raising up of Saul at Endor does testify to a widespread belief in the survival of human ghosts, it is clear that that belief did not occupy a central place in the Bible's religious consciousness. As Yehezkel Kaufmann characterizes the situation: "That the spirit of the deceased lives on apart from the body is the belief of the people, but biblical faith draws no religious or moral inferences from this notion."[4] The afterlife is at most a fact of nature that carries no visible implications as regards one's moral or religious behavior. Death will not bring the individual closer to God, nor will the afterlife be the setting for eternal rewards or punishments. Neither the ritual nor the moral precepts of the Torah are commanded with a view to preparing people for life in the hereafter.

Most modern historical scholarship has assumed that the Israelite popular religion postulated a more tangible and active survival of the soul in an underworld. This view is usually supported by citing cultural comparisons with neighboring peoples, archeological remnants of local burial practices, and by noting the vehemence with which necromancy was condemned by the Torah. If these beliefs were so prevalent among the common people, then it is remarkable that they receive so little mention in the Bible. Scholars have generally ascribed this fact to a conscious policy of the biblical redactors, the formulators of the "official" religion of Israel, who emphasized the absolute value of life in the present world and insisted that people (themselves or their descendants) would receive earthly retribution for their deeds.[5] The most reasonable explanation for this antagonism to afterlife ideas appears to be Kaufmann's, that afterlife conceptions in the ancient Near East were invariably connected with deification of the deceased or of the rulers of the underworld, and hence were perceived as inherently antithetical to the prophetic ideal of monotheism.

BABYLONIAN EXILE AND SECOND COMMONWEALTH (539 B.C.E. to 70 C.E.)[6]

The stability of the First Commonwealth gave way to turmoil and national disaster. First the ten tribes of the northern Kingdom of Israel were conquered by the Assyrians and sent to an exile from which they would never be regathered. Afterward, Nebuchadnezzar's Babylonian armies invaded Judea, destroying Solomon's Temple and deporting the population. However, when Babylonia fell to Persia, a remnant of the Judeans responded to the call of the Persian emperor Cyrus to return to Jerusalem, rebuild their Temple, and resume their cultural and religious life.

The harsh realities of everyday life would gradually have eroded people's confidence in seeing justice in this world. The terrible national catastrophes made it even harder to accept the claim that history provides satisfactory retribution for the righteous and the wicked. In contrast to the earlier belief in transgenerational corporate responsibility, a new sense of individual accountability was voiced by post-Exilic prophets. Jeremiah and Ezekiel asserted that individuals are judged only for their own iniquities, not for those of their ancestors. Probably around this time the author of the Book of Job struggled with the issue of the undeserved suffering of the righteous, rejecting facile apologetics but ultimately unable to penetrate God's inscrutable ways. Although the literary remains of the Exilic and early Second Commonwealth eras attest to a questioning of the traditional rationales, the writers of this era did not propose that life's inequities would be rectified in the hereafter.[7]

We possess almost no records of Jewish religious thought during the Persian period, from the early days of the Second Commonwealth through to the encounter with Hellenism in the late fourth century B.C.E. However, as soon as we emerge from this historical "dark age" it becomes evident that one particular conception of the afterlife had become widespread in Jewish circles: the belief in the bodily resurrection of the dead. The origins of this idea are shrouded in obscurity. Most historians believe that the notions of resurrection and judgment in the afterlife were imported into Judaism from Persian Zoroastrianism.[8] Although later generations would trace the idea back to Ezekiel's symbolic vision of the Valley of the Dry Bones (37:1–14), where the revival of lifeless skeletons symbolized the miraculous redemption of the scattered and dispirited Jewish nation, the passage furnishes evidence that belief in individual resurrection was not widely held, for when God asks Ezekiel "Can these bones live?" the prophet is unable to give a lucid answer—hardly the appropriate response if resurrection were the normative belief.

Jewish texts from the early second century onward, including works that are not normally perceived as emanating from narrow sectarian circles, speak of resurrection as the ultimate fate of the deceased. The Book of Daniel, composed in the shadow of the persecutions of Antiochos IV Epiphanes (ca. 165), promises that "many of them that sleep in the dust shall awake, some to everlasting life and some to shame and everlasting contempt" (12:2–3). The author of 2 Maccabees, which recounts the successful Jewish revolt against the Hellenistic oppressors, tells of Jewish soldiers who contributed toward the purchase of sin-offerings on behalf of comrades who had died while still tainted by sin, commending them for "acting very finely and properly in taking account of the resurrection" (12:43–45). The long-winded justification of their action suggests that resurrection was still a controversial idea.

We can appreciate how a belief in an afterlife would satisfy a natural human craving for immortality and provide an effective incentive for martyrdom in times of persecution (Maccabees) or a scenario for just and final retribution (Daniel). However, it is not immediately apparent why these authors should have opted for a conception of *bodily* survival rather than some form of *spiritual* immortality. We are probably justified in regarding its wide acceptance among Jews as a rejection of the prevalent Greek attitudes, which denigrated physical existence as being antithetical to humanity's proper rational vocation.[9] By insisting that even in death we will continue to inhabit physical bodies the proponents of resurrection were underscoring the inherent sanctity of material creation, in keeping with the attitudes of biblical religion. Furthermore, although the continuing existence of a soul or intellect can be perceived as a "natural" process independent of faith in a God (as in some modern parapsychological theories), it is impossible to imagine a *reversal* of nature, such as the reconstitution of decomposed flesh, except through miraculous divine intervention. Some scholars have argued that from its beginnings the teaching of bodily resurrection was intimately connected with its role in eschatological visions (see below).[10]

Sources emanating from the first century C.E.—including the historian Josephus Flavius, the Christian gospels, Jewish Rabbinic traditions—are in rare agreement when they depict the issue of afterlife conceptions as a pivotal topic of sectarian dispute among the three main Jewish "philosophies" of the late Second Commonwealth. In Josephus's famous accounts of the three Jewish parties we read that the Pharisees proclaimed the eternity of the soul, asserting that the dead are judged "under the earth." The righteous pass on to other bodies, while the wicked are condemned to eternal punishment or "imprisonment." In stating that the wicked are denied resurrection altogether, it is evident that Josephus's Pharisees are at variance with the author of Daniel, for whom judgment takes place *after* the resurrection. As for Josephus's apparent suggestion that we are dealing with *transmigration* or *reincarnation* (perhaps into an unborn body) rather than *resurrection* (to a reconstituted version of one's original body), most scholars believe that we should not attach too much weight to this detail, since Josephus frequently introduces formulations of this sort in order to conform to categories that were familiar to his Greek readership. The second major Jewish movement, the priestly Sadducees, rejected all conceptions of survival after death or of retribution beyond the grave.

This dispute is consistent with the general characters of the two groups. The Sadducees, "fundamentalists" who acknowledged no religious authority outside the Bible, were continuing the biblical eschewal of afterlife conceptions. The Pharisees, on the other hand, were famous for their reverence for ancestral traditions that were passed down orally among the folk. The successors to the Pharisees during the Talmudic era would formulate a theology according to which such traditions had been revealed to Moses at Mount Sinai (though the idea of resurrection had evidently achieved currency only since the Persian era).

Josephus's description of the third Jewish movement, the Essenes, equates their opinion with that of Greek philosophy, that the body is a prison-house that drags the soul down during a person's lifetime, until death provides a liberating release for the virtuous souls, who will dwell eternally in a paradise "beyond the ocean." As in the view ascribed to the Pharisees, the souls that prove unworthy of such a blessed destiny will be consigned to ceaseless torment. Since we possess no other explicit evidence of the Essene position on this question, we are unable to evaluate the accuracy of Josephus's description, though we might assume that he has again Hellenized his account. Significantly, there do not appear to be any texts among the Qumran documents (the "Dead Sea Scrolls" commonly attributed to the Essenes) that reflect such a view of the afterlife.[11]

Other texts from the Second Commonwealth present a complex assortment of attitudes towards human immortality and the afterlife. The pre-Maccabean Ben-Sira (Ecclesiasticus) maintained the conservative, Sadducee-like belief in death's finality. The Hellenized Philo of Alexandria extolled the immortality of the soul and mind, but not of the despised physical body. Apocalyptic authors offered graphic descriptions of the terrible retribution in store for God's enemies. Jesus of Nazareth defended the Pharisaic position (on his own terms, to be sure) against Sadducee antagonists, and his followers believed that Jesus himself underwent resurrection, though the early church was not always certain what implications to draw from this belief. Even

Josephus is not always consistent in distinguishing between bodily resurrection and survival of the soul, and whether such souls abide in "heaven" or under the earth.

TALMUDIC PERSPECTIVES (70 to ca. 700 C.E.)[12]

The Great Rebellion against Rome culminated in 70 C.E. with the destruction of Judaism's cherished sanctuary and the eradication of Jewish political autonomy. Of the sects that had fragmented Jewish religious life during the latter days of the Second Commonwealth, only the Pharisees appear to have survived the catastrophe, and many of their ideas now became features of a Jewish consensus. The religious teachings of the Jewish sages (now known as Rabbis) would eventually be compiled into several unwritten compendia of which the most prominent were the Mishnah, the Palestinian and Babylonian Talmuds, and numerous collections of biblical interpretation (Midrash), which could be either legal (*halakhic*) or homiletical (*aggadic*).

In spite of the Rabbis' usual reluctance to impose mandatory creeds, a passage in the Mishnah (Sanhedrin 10:1) enumerates "one who denies the resurrection of the dead" among the heretics who forfeit their place in the world to come. The "world to come" was one of several new terms that were introduced in the Rabbinic discussions of the subject. A blessing praising God as "the reviver of the dead" was incorporated into the daily Jewish liturgy.

It is rare for Rabbinic theological ideas to be formulated systematically, and therefore their details must often be inferred from the homiletical or exegetical contexts in which they appear. Since Rabbinic literature was a collective enterprise, spanning some six centuries in both Babylonia and the Land of Israel, we cannot always assume that the diverse comments preserved in the literature are susceptible to harmonization. Of the topics that we shall survey in this section, some seem to result from serious reflection on the implications of the basic concepts; some were inspired by scriptural texts; others probably arose from homiletical motives, as incentives to virtuous behavior; and still others were products of the unrestrained folk imagination.

Whatever ambivalence might have attached to Josephus's descriptions of the resurrection process, Rabbinic works are quite clear that the dead will be restored to their own bodies, not to unborn[13] or existing ones. Since observation tells us that this does not occur immediately after death, it was natural that the process should be projected to an unspecified future age. This led to the integration of resurrection into the complex array of Jewish beliefs about ultimate redemption and restoration under the leadership of the anointed Son of David, the Messiah. Bringing the dead back to life was perceived as a stage in the Jewish eschatological vision, one of the many wonders that would be performed in the redeemed world.[14]

Rabbinic sources often refer to the destination of the departed as the "World to Come," a term that usually referred to their state after the Messianic resurrection.[15] The question naturally arose of what befalls the souls between the moments of death and resurrection. A widespread notion held that the disembodied spirits continue to live on as individuals in a supernatural abode (see below), and several texts seem to apply the term "World to Come" to the place souls inhabit immediately after separation from their bodies.[16]

Without completely abandoning the biblical notions of divine retribution in this life, the Rabbis came to realize that neither the righteous nor the wicked receive full compensation in their lifetimes. The sense of dissatisfaction was heightened during the Hadrianic persecutions of 132-35, when Jews often suffered horrible martyrdom at the hands of the Romans precisely because they had maintained their devotion to their religion. Faith in divine justice demanded that a more equitable settling of accounts should await both the martyrs and their tormentors.[17]

The literature of the Second Commonwealth had dealt with similar questions, and no unified picture emerged of when and how the judgment would take place. We have already noted the discrepancy between Daniel and Josephus's Pharisees about whether the unrighteous will experience resurrection at all. Several texts from that period envisage some separation and punishment of the wicked, at least in a preliminary form, while in the grave.[18] The Mishnah, in denying heretics and sinners "a portion in the World to Come," seems to reflect Josephus's view, but our sources preserve a variety of approaches to the question.

In Rabbinic speculations about the fates of the righteous and sinners, the souls of the former inhabit the "Garden of Eden" whereas the latter suffer torments in "Gehenna." In the Bible, the Garden of Eden had been an idyllic paradise from which the first woman and man had been expelled after disobeying God. Although some Rabbinic sources can be interpreted as referring to a terrestrial site, most seem to speak of a supernatural, "heavenly" paradise. The name Gehinom is usually traced to the "Vale [Hebrew: *Gei*] of Ben Hinom" south of Jerusalem, which had been a notorious site of a child-sacrifice cult during the First Commonwealth.[19] Not surprisingly, the popular imagination supplied tangible graphic descriptions of both afterlife destinations. Much of the material now embodied in Rabbinic literature originated in sermons that were preached in the ancient synagogues, in which context vivid depictions of Paradise and Gehenna provide effective incentives for pursuing good and eschewing evil.

Although the elaborate Rabbinic beliefs about the afterlife strike us as departures from the biblical outlook summarized above, the Rabbis themselves acknowledged no discrepancies between scriptural religion and their own, and hence applied their exegetical skills (as embodied in the sophisticated methods of midrash) to uncovering afterlife references beneath the surfaces of the biblical verses. Interpretations of this sort were often stimulated by polemics with dissenting or heretical ideologies within Judaism or outside it.

The belief in physical resurrection carried practical implications with respect to the care of corpses. Because the physical remains will one day be restored to life, they may not be destroyed.[20] Therefore burial is the only sanctioned way of disposing of a corpse, and to arrange a proper burial was esteemed as a pious manifestation of the honor due to the dead.

Aside from the major themes outlined in the preceding paragraphs, Rabbinic literature is replete with whimsical speculations concerning every conceivable aspect of the hereafter. Issues discussed in the pages of the Talmud and Midrash include: Are the dead cognizant of what goes on among mortals? Will people be resurrected naked or clothed? What will happen to those whose bodies were maimed and crippled?

MEDIEVAL JUDAISM (ca. 700 to ca. 1750 C.E.)

In many respects the Jewish "Middle Ages" were a continuation and consolidation of patterns that were established during the Talmudic era. However, two new interpretations of Judaism arose at this time, each with its own novel perspectives on the afterlife.

RATIONALISM[21]

Jews of Arab-speaking lands shared in the rediscovery of the Greek philosophical heritage that began when the Muslim conquerors of Syria were exposed to Syriac translations of Plato, Aristotle, and others. We shall confine ourselves here to a sampling of the more influential formulations of medieval Jewish rationalism.

A limited rationalistic influence can be discerned among "theologians" who invoked reason not as the ultimate arbiter of religious truth but only as an aid to maintaining order amid the disarray of the received tradition. In the Islamic world this theological endeavor was known as *Kalam*, a term modern scholars commonly extend to its Jewish equivalents.

A notable representative was the tenth-century Rabbi Saadia *Ga'on.*[22] In his *Book of Doctrines and Opinions* Saadia integrated the Rabbinic afterlife ideas into a broader constellation of theological issues, including the reasons for the creation of the universe and of humanity, free will and moral accountability, the nature of the soul, theodicy, good and evil. Saadia provided additional rational support for the received beliefs in the afterlife (which he inferred from the absence of divine justice in the present world) and resurrection. Like many rationalists, he interpreted the sensuous midrashic images of Paradise and Gehenna as metaphors for spiritual states. Aware of the ambiguities in the Rabbinic uses of the term "World to Come," he opted for a metaphysical rather than an eschatological understanding, and argued that the initial resurrection in the Messianic era will include only Israel, whereas the righteous of all nations will be revived in the World to Come.

In the Greek tradition the prevailing model for immortality derived from the eternity of abstract ideas. The truths of logic and metaphysics, because they are immune from the corruptibility of physical matter, will persist for all time. Human beings can partake of eternity to the degree that they are capable of contemplating abstract verities. Medieval Jewish rationalists read that concept of impersonal immortality into the traditional Rabbinic imagery.

In the cosmology of the Jewish Aristotelians (as exemplified in the oeuvre of their most illustrious representative, the twelfth-century Egyptian scholar Moses Maimonides), a sequence of emanated "Separate Intelligences," pure disembodied intellects, occupies the continuum between God and our world, equated with the biblical angels and with the astronomical bodies that orbit the earth. The lowest of these, the "Active Intellect," is the power that imprints upon the human mind (initially only a "potential intellect") the capacity to conceptualize universal and abstract ideas that are not merely collections of sense-data. The influence of the Active Intellect on the human mind produces the "Acquired Intellect," which is the only part of the human being that remains immortal. Since this "immortality" is equated with participation in universal truth, the Jewish philosophers were not in agreement about whether people retain their individuality or are subsumed into a cosmic intellect.[23]

This conception is a far cry from the traditional biblical and Rabbinic ideas. It makes immortality contingent upon rational rather than moral perfection. At best, morality and observance of the Torah serve as a *means* for achieving the intellectual objectives by providing the material conditions for philosophizing or by disciplining the mind to resist the distractions of the "bodily appetites." Ultimately, however, it remains an elitist ideal, accessible only to those who possess the requisite intellectual gifts and training. Some of the Jewish philosophers tried to mitigate these objections by observing that the Torah provides the most efficient pedagogic means for elevating large numbers of people to the appropriate intellectual levels. Maimonides's "Thirteen Articles of Creed" defined minimal levels of intellectual attainment that are accessible to the less sophisticated.

With their disdain for everything physical and corruptible the rationalists found themselves at odds with the traditional faith in the restoration of the physical body. Although Maimonides enumerated belief in resurrection among the mandatory Jewish dogmas, his sincerity was questioned by some contemporaries, and he composed a special treatise to confirm his commitment to the doctrine. However, it is evident that resurrection occupies, at most, an incidental place in Maimonides's eschatology: it will occur in the Messianic era, but the revived persons will die natural deaths and afterward enjoy true spiritual bliss in a nonphysical World to Come.[24]

KABBALAH[25]

The medieval esoteric theosophy known as the Kabbalah was built upon a distinctive theory of ten divine creative powers known as *sefirot*, which serve as intermediaries between the unknowable God and the created world. Kabbalah combines speculative theology, a program of religious observance, and novel methods of biblical interpretation into a complex mystical restatement of traditional Judaism. The foremost literary creation of the Kabbalah was the *Zohar*, the *Book of Splendor*, a pseudepigraphic collection of homiletical discourses on the Bible believed to have been composed in the late thirteenth century by Rabbi Moses de Leon of Guadalajara, Spain. Some important Kabbalistic movements include the circle of Rabbi Isaac Luria in sixteenth-century Safed, and the Eastern European populist Hasidic movement which arose in the late eighteenth century.

The Kabbalists discerned at least three different components in the human soul.[26] This psychological theory allowed them to resolve some of the discrepancies between earlier afterlife conceptions. Accordingly, it is only the lowliest, animal soul (*nefesh*) that endures punishment in the grave. The spirit (*ruaḥ*) is eventually admitted to the "earthly Garden of Eden," whereas the immaculate soul (*neshamah*), originating in the supernal *sefirot* and in the universal soul of the primordial Adam, ultimately returns to its divine source in the "celestial Garden of Eden." In the more radical versions of the theory, the *neshamah* was perceived as a part of God that is being restored to its source. This raised questions of whether souls retain individual personalities in the hereafter.

Kabbalah was the only Jewish movement for which the transmigration of souls (*gilgul*)[27] was the normative afterlife doctrine, a notion they often combined with belief in the preexistence of souls. One popular theory spoke of each soul fashioning a spiritual garment composed of virtuous deeds, which it will don when it is finally admitted to God's presence. Early Kabbalists envisaged metempsychosis as a punishment, or second chance, for certain transgressions (especially sexual ones). However, later sources treat it as a normal process, which is not necessarily restricted to human bodies. Various authors disagreed over specifics; for example, how many times can a person be reincarnated? Why is there need for punishment both through reincarnation and through the fires of Gehenna?

Variations on the transmigration motif include the belief that a departed soul can enter ("impregnate") a living person to fulfill certain missions. Kabbalistic folklore often spoke of possession (*dibbuk*) by sinful spirits who had forfeited their right to redemptive transmigration.

MODERN JUDAISM (from ca. 1750)[28]

Since the admission of Jews to full participation in European society exposed them to contemporary intellectual currents, Jewish theology has been distinguished less by its promulgation of original ideas than by its varying degrees of resistance or receptivity to outside (usually Christian) concepts.

Acknowledgment of the principle of physical resurrection continues to be a defining feature of traditional ("Orthodox") Judaism, reinforced by avowals in the daily liturgy. The Talmudic doctrine is usually interpreted through its classic medieval formulations, whether philosophical (especially the Maimonidean version) or Kabbalistic (Isaac Luria's teachings continue to exercise strong influences on the Hasidic movement and in Oriental Jewish communities).

The Jewish Reform movement, which developed in central and western Europe during the eighteenth and nineteenth centuries, professed both a rejection of Rabbinic authority and a determination to conform to the social needs and cultural climate of modern Europe. From both these perspectives, literal belief in resurrection was generally considered unacceptable. Liberal Protestants, who often spoke in the name of universalistic enlightenment, preferred a model of spiritual immortality, and many "enlightened" and liberal Jews shared the conviction that immortality of the soul is rationally demonstrable.[29]

Discussions of the afterlife are almost entirely absent from non-Orthodox twentieth-century religious discourse, which has focused on the absolute commitment to this world as the setting for the encounter with the divine, the covenant between God and Israel, and the obligation to serve humanity.[30] Even Franz Rosenzweig (1886–1929), whose theology was responding to the challenges of human mortality, conceived of eternity as a religious dimension of *life*, not as an afterlife state. Similarly, the important theological responses to the Nazi Holocaust, as formulated by authors like Elie Wiesel, Emil Fackenheim, Richard Rubinstein, and others, have been rendered more poignant and painful by their reluctance to appeal to a supernatural retribution in a World to Come.

Notes

[1] Works cited in this section include Yehezkel Kaufmann, *The Religion of Israel: From Its Beginnings to the Babylonian Exile* (Chicago: University of Chicago Press, 1960); Hans Walter Wolff, *Anthropology of the Old Testament*, trans. Margaret Kohl (Philadelphia: Fortress

Press, 1974), pp. 100–6; Johannes Pedersen, *Israel: Its Life and Culture* (London and Copenhagen: Oxford University Press and Branner og Korch, 1973), pp. 460–70. Thanks to Dr. Michael DeRoche for directing me to useful references.

[2] S. G. F. Brandon, *Man and His Destiny in the Great Religions* (Manchester: Manchester University Press, 1972), pp. 116–17, attaches importance to 1 Samuel 25:29, where Abigail blesses David saying, "Yet the soul of my lord shall be bound in the bundle of the living with the Lord thy God; and the souls of thine enemies, them shall he sling out." However, "soul" might serve here as an equivalent to "life," so that the text would mean that God will preserve David's life but quickly cast down his enemies.

[3] "The etymology of [*she'ol*] is still obscure. . . . Friedrich Delitzsch identified it with a supposed Babylonian term *shu'âlu*. But this view has long since been abandoned" (Alexander Heidel, *The Gilgamesh Epic and Old Testament Parallels* [Chicago: University of Chicago Press, 1965], p. 173).

[4] Kaufmann, p. 311.

[5] E.g., Wayne Pitard, "Afterlife and Immortality," in *The Oxford Companion to the Bible*, ed. Bruce Metzger and Michael Coogan (Oxford: Oxford University Press, 1993), pp. 15–16. Brandon (pp. 118–29) regards the "Yahwist" antipathy to afterlife ideas as a byproduct of their attempt to replace local tribal cults with a centralized national religion.

[6] Works that deal with afterlife conceptions during this period include Brandon, pp. 129–50; Salo Baron, *A Social and Religious History of the Jews* (New York: Columbia University Press, 1962–), 1:135–38, 357; 2:38–41, 345; Shaye D. Cohen, *From the Maccabees to the Mishnah* (Philadelphia: Westminster Press, 1987); George Foot Moore, *Judaism in the First Centuries of the Christian Era* (Cambridge: Harvard University Press, 1958), 2:279–322, 88–92; G. Nickelsburg, *Resurrection, Immortality and Eternal Life in Intertestamental Judaism* (1972); E. P. Sanders, *Judaism Practice and Belief* (London and Philadelphia: SCM Press and Trinity Press International, 1992), pp. 298–303; Emil Schürer, *The History of the Jewish People in the Age of Jesus Christ*, rev. G. Vermes et al. (Edinburgh: Clark, 1979), 2:391–92, 539–47.

[7] The author of Ecclesiastes ironically described how death renders futile all human achievement.

[8] Shaul Shaked, "Iranian Influence on Judaism," in *The Cambridge History of Judaism*, ed. W. D. Davies and Louis Finkelstein (Cambridge: Cambridge University Press, 1984–), 1:308–25.

[9] Hellenistic Jewish thinkers like Philo of Alexandria and the author of the Wisdom of Solomon speak disparagingly of the body as weighing down the soul (see Brandon, pp. 141–43; Sanders, pp. 298–99).

[10] See Schürer, pp. 391–92, 537–40.

[11] The survival of disembodied souls is mentioned in Enoch and Jubilees, works that occupy prominent places in the Qumran library (see Schürer, p. 539, n. 90 and p. 5, n. 93).

[12] I am aware of no full-scale monograph on afterlife conceptions during the Talmudic era. Much information can be gleaned from the pertinent index entries in Louis Ginzberg, *The Legends of the Jews* (Philadelphia: Jewish Publication Society, 1967).

[13] Talmudic sources know of a Platonic-like idea of the *pre-existent* souls (see Ephraim Urbach, *The Sages* [Cambridge Mass.: Harvard University Press, 1987], pp. 235-48).

[14] This view is also found in apocalyptical works like 4 Ezra (7:31–34) (see Schürer, p. 539).

[15] H. Albeck, *Shishah Sidrei Mishnah* (Jerusalem and Tel-Aviv: Bialik Institute and Dvir, 1959), 4:454.

[16] Louis Finkelstein, *Mabo le-Massektot Abot ve-Abot d'Rabbi Natan* (New York: Jewish Theological Seminary, 1950), pp. 212–20; Max Kadushin, *The Rabbinic Mind* (New York: Bloch, 1972), pp. 361-64.

[17] Urbach, pp. 436–44.

[18] Schürer, pp. 540–41.

[19] See especially Jeremiah 7:32–33. S. Klein has suggested that some of the Rabbinic references might have originally been to the "Vale of Hamon" in Transjordan, site of a hot spring whose underground source was popularly linked to the flames of Hell ("*Ha'naḥotei' verabbah bar bar ḥana*," *Me'assef Zion* 5 [1933], pp. 1–13).

[20] The issue is obviously symbolic. The God who can reconstitute decomposed flesh is surely able to reassemble dispersed ashes.

[21] Standard surveys of medieval Jewish philosophy include Julius Guttmann, *Philosophies of Judaism* (New York: Schocken, 1973); Isaac Husik, *A History of Medieval Jewish Philosophy* (New York: Harper & Row, 1966); Colette Sirat, *A History of Jewish Philosophy in the Middle Ages* (Cambridge and Paris: Cambridge University Press and Maison des Sciences de l'Homme, 1985).

[22] Guttmann, pp. 82–83; Husik, pp. 41–47; Sirat, pp. 33–35.

[23] Guttmann, pp. 152–59, 176–78, 199–207; Husik, pp. xxxiv–xlvii; Sirat, pp. 170–71, 187–88, 203.

[24] Guttmann, pp. 208–9; Sirat, pp. 170–72.

[25] Material related to this section is collected in Gerschom Scholem, *Kabbalah* (New York: New American Library, 1978).

[26] Scholem, pp. 155–65.

[27] Scholem, pp. 347-50.

[28] Useful summaries include Guttmann; Eugene Borowitz, *Choices in Modern Jewish Thought* (New York: Behrman House, 1983); Simon Noveck, ed., *Great Jewish Thinkers of the Twentieth Century* (Clinton: B'nai Brith, 1963).

[29] This was maintained by otherwise diverse thinkers like the traditionalist Moses Mendelssohn (1729-86), the pioneer of Jewish Enlightenment, and the liberal Solomon Steinheim (1789-1866).

[30] This is true of such well-known Jewish existentialists as Martin Buber, Abraham Heschel, and others. An articulate exception is Louis Jacobs, *A Jewish Theology* (New York: Behrman House, 1973), pp. 319-22.

2

Christianity

Terence Penelhum

Christianity is unique among the world's religions in the nature of the claims it makes about its founder. He is seen not merely as a teacher or example, but as someone whose life and death are accorded a cosmic significance that holds the key to the cure of the deepest ills of the human condition. Christianity's central doctrines are attempts to spell out this significance. Since Christianity entered a culture deeply influenced by Greek thought, which had reached a highly advanced form before Christianity appeared, it absorbed many of the ideas of that culture, even though its relationship to it was, and is, an uneasy one.[1] Its claims about the afterlife are typical in this respect.

CHRISTIAN ORIGINS

The Christian movement began with Jesus preaching in Galilee: "The Kingdom of God is at hand; repent and believe the good news." The language of this proclamation was familiar to his Jewish hearers: God's Kingdom, or rule, was something they longed for after years of foreign (by then Roman) domination, and they thought of it as a transformation of their life that God would one day bring about, probably suddenly and dramatically.

Jesus proclaimed that this was about to happen, and that his hearers should prepare for it by changing their way of life radically in order to fit themselves for citizenship in God's Kingdom. This message of itself did not make him so different from the Pharisees, for example; what he said about the requirements for entry into the Kingdom made him different.

In the first place, those he said would enter were not those one naturally would expect to enter. The Kingdom is not for the rich but for the poor. It is not for the scribes and the teachers but for the ignorant and the children. It is not for those who have conscientiously kept themselves righteous but for the tax-gatherers and the prostitutes whom the righteous have avoided. Entry is for those listed in the Beatitudes. But this does not mean that the demands of the Kingdom are easy ones. On the contrary: the ethics of the Kingdom are more rigorous than the ethics of the Jewish Law. It is not good enough that you do not have sexual relations with your neighbor's wife; you must not even want to. It is not good enough that you do not murder; you must not even hate. The Kingdom is for the pure in heart. What the Kingdom demands is inner reformation. If you have achieved this inner reformation, you will, to put it in a single phrase, act out of love of God and of others and will not be so concerned about following rules.

Acting out of love is acting for the good of others without asking whether they deserve it. None of us does. The Kingdom is not a realm where people get what they deserve, but where they act toward each other without considering that. The command to forgive, for example, is just a simple application of this. The citizens of the Kingdom will not protect themselves from one another. The trouble with the people who have always followed the rules is that they have done this as a protection, to be accounted righteous.

This prompts an objection. To act from love is to put myself at risk. Why should I? The answer is that I should do this because God treats me that way; God showers benefits on me without regard to my merits, and that is why I should act in the same way. But this prompts another objection. That is all very well for God, for this is God's world. But if I act like that, I might be cheated or passed by or injured or killed. How can I overcome my fear of all these things; indeed why *should* I overcome it? Isn't the ethic of the Kingdom utopian and imprudent?

The answer is no. If you really believe that you are a child of God, then you will be completely confident that God will see to it that your needs will be satisfied, and you will then not be anxious. If you do not believe this, love toward your neighbor is indeed foolish and hazardous. But if you do believe it (if you trust God), then you will be able to put your anxieties aside and act from love.

This means that to be prepared for the Kingdom when it comes, you have to think, feel, and act *now* as though it is here already. And then, paradoxically, it will be. Or, at least, a nucleus of it will be. This is why we find so many references to the Kingdom that speak of it not as coming but as actually here. The community of Christ and his disciples is a nucleus that will, through God's agency, grow like the mustard seed.

These features of Jesus' early preaching reveal something that is central to the understanding of the role played by the belief in an afterlife in the Christian tradition. Jesus' ethical teaching takes place in a context in which his hearers are told that God is in control of their lives and is poised to transform their world, and that his hearers must turn toward God and act without reservation in the ways he demands. So the demands of the present are expressed in ways that make the sense they do because of his expectations of the future. If you do not share those expectations, the demands are hopelessly idealistic and psychologically impossible to satisfy. There is a crucial connection between Jesus' ethics and his eschatology.

But to speak merely of Jesus' proclamations of the imminence of God's Kingdom is to leave out many essentials of Christian doctrine about his significance. It is clear from the gospel texts that even in these proclamations Jesus claimed a special authority, a right to speak for God and to interpret the Jewish tradition in which he stood. It is also clear that this claim was resisted and rejected by the authorities he challenged. Whether or not his own understanding of his role changed, it is clear that he came in time to speak of himself as having a central place not merely in the preparation of his followers for the coming of the Kingdom, but in its actual arrival in final form. He appears to have accepted the judgment of his disciples that he was indeed the Messiah, the anointed figure most Jews expected to deliver them. But he did not see this role as one of political victory but rather one of suffering and death. He accordingly went up to Jerusalem, where he engaged in the series of confrontations with Jewish authorities that led to his arrest and execution. The gospels portray his execution as a judicial murder in which the Jewish authorities represented him to the Romans as a political revolutionary. The passion narratives of the Christian scriptures make it abundantly clear that this wholly unjust political death was one which Jesus in no way resisted but saw as God's appointed destiny for him.

Jesus' followers went into hiding. But a very short time afterward they burst again upon the scene, saying that he had risen from the dead, that he had appeared to them, that he had empowered them to proclaim him as Messiah and Lord, and that he would return in glory to bring the Kingdom of God to its completion. The community they formed spread rapidly, to become over the centuries the Christian church as we know it. The doctrines of that church are its attempts to understand and represent to the world the full significance of these events.

The Evolution of Christian Doctrine

By far the most important formulation of Christian doctrines is that found in the writings of St. Paul, a Pharisee who began by persecuting the Christian community but was converted to it very dramatically and became its most famous missionary and its first theologian. His letters, which were written well before any of the gospels, are intensely controversial documents that spell out the significance of Christ (the Greek word for Messiah) in the face of challenges and misinterpretations. It is Pauline theology that has determined the bounds of orthodoxy for Christians ever since.

Paul was a preacher to the Gentiles (non-Jews), and in his hands Christianity ceased to be a Jewish sect and became universal in its claims. So Jesus' sacrificial death was a means of salvation for all people. But Paul still sees it in terms of the anthropology of the Hebrew scriptures. Every one of us is in a state of corruption, or sin, which has come about through the fact that our earliest ancestors, Adam and Eve, disobeyed God. We all inherit their rebellious state, and the inherited moral corruption is the source of our physical corruption, that is, of death. We are able to recognize that we are sinful, and we may well want to reform ourselves and turn back to God; but we do not have the inner power, of ourselves, to make this change. The role of Christ is to reconcile us to God and to give us this power. His death, unlike ours, was not a consequence of sin; it was wholly unmerited. In raising him from the dead, God has proclaimed that those who repent and accept Christ will be forgiven. This will not spare them from dying, but it will give them the reassurance that they will be raised as Christ was and be spared from corruption.

This is the core of Christian theology. It proclaims that the church is the interim Kingdom of God and looks forward to a time when God's Kingdom will reach consummation: a completion that is thought of by Paul and his successors as entailing resurrection from the dead, a prediction guaranteed for us by the resurrection of Christ. The early fathers of the church, reflecting on the implications of this saving message and anxious to avoid importing alien interpretations into it, drew from it two central doctrines that all Christians since have acknowledged on pain of heresy: the doctrine of the Incarnation (that only a being who was fully divine as well as human could make the saving sacrifice Jesus made) and the doctrine of the Trinity (that the relation among God the Father, who creates, God the Son, who saves, and God the Holy Spirit, who empowers and sanctifies, is an eternal combination of identity and distinctness). I can say nothing here about the vast problems to which these doctrines give rise, but I will try to relate the core Christian proclamation to the belief in life after death.

Jewish and Christian Beliefs about the Hereafter

As the first Christians were Jews, their understanding of the significance of Jesus' life and death was conditioned by their Jewish heritage. It is frequently said that the Hebrew religious tradition is centered on God's relationship to the whole people of Israel and that there is little concern in it for issues of individual survival. This is clearly true, but it has to be modified when we come to consider the religious thought of the Jews in the time of Jesus. Early or classical Judaism saw death as the end of any meaningful form of life or relationship to God. The dead did not become wholly extinct, however, but entered the underworld, known as Sheol. The inhabitants of Sheol are called *rephaim*, whom we can refer to perhaps as "shades." Their mode of existence is dim, lethargic, and unenviable; they are cut off from the fullness of life as it is known to those still in the body. But dimness and lethargy are not the same as sheer nonexistence; and the *rephaim* appear to have been thought of as somehow identical with the individuals whose psychical relics they are.

Two other elements in Hebrew thought about the afterlife are relevant to our theme. The first is the later emergence of an expectation that immediately after death each person will be judged and his or her spirit will join those who are saved and destined for happiness or those who are condemned. For those who held this expectation, Sheol became the abode not of all the spirits but only of the condemned; it evolved, as it were, into Gehenna, a place of torment and burning. This picture of the afterlife is found in the famous story of the rich man and Lazarus (Lk 16:19-31).

The second theme that had clearly emerged by New Testament times and is reported there as dividing the Jewish community is the expectation of resurrection. There are only a small number of proof-texts on this in the Hebrew scriptures; the clearest are in Isaiah 26:19 and Daniel 12:2. There are other "intertestamental" texts, such as the Book of Enoch, that also teach a future resurrection. These texts speak of those who are asleep in the earth being raised, and the Isaiah text, at least, clearly envisages a *bodily* existence in the future for those who are raised. This expectation was associated with the hope and vision of God's final deliverance and restoration of God's people, and means that the righteous dead will be brought back to life again to share in the restored Kingdom.

These teachings do not fit together easily or harmoniously, and they were clearly intensely controversial among the Jews themselves. The Sadducees rejected all forms of future life; the Pharisees accepted the belief in the resurrection. On this matter Jesus clearly took their side and is recorded as refuting the Sadducees in Mark 12:18-27. He is also recorded as saying things that imply the reality of an afterlife immediately following death, one in which the dead are divided by some sort of judgment (see Lk 16:19-31, 23:39-43).

THE CORE CHRISTIAN CLAIMS ABOUT THE AFTERLIFE

The primary sources for these are Paul's letters, which were written before the resurrection narratives in the four gospels and contain the direct claim by the writer himself that he was a witness to one of Jesus' appearances. What Paul says is by far the fullest statement in the Christian scriptures of what believers may hope for. The longest and most important Pauline text is 1 Corinthians 15.

Paul seems to have written this letter to respond to some Christians in Corinth who had come to doubt whether there was to be a resurrection. They may have been influenced here by Greek philosophical thinking. Whatever reasons they had, Paul begins his response to them by insisting that the resurrection is the core of his proclamation: the salvation Christians inherit is a consequence of the fact that Jesus was raised from the dead, and this entails that they, too, will be raised. Without *both*, the faith is empty and "those who have died within Christ's fellowship are utterly lost" (v. 18).[2] Christ *was* raised, and Paul lists a series of public post-resurrection appearances where Jesus met his followers. The last such appearance, he says, was to himself. All readers interpret this as having been his dramatic conversion experience on the road to Damascus. He describes the risen Christ as "the firstfruits of the harvest of the dead" (v. 20). Next come the famous dramatic sentences: "As in Adam all men die, so in Christ all will be brought to life; but each in his own proper place: Christ the firstfruits, and afterwards, at his coming, those who belong to Christ. Then comes the end, when he delivers up the kingdom to God the Father, after abolishing every kind of domination, authority, and power. For he is destined to reign until God has put all enemies under his feet; and the last enemy to be abolished is death" (vv. 22-27).

So Christ will return, and when he does those who belong to him will be raised and all will be subjected to him. Paul then turns to the natural question of what sort of body those who are raised from the dead will have. He says, first, that this is a foolish question. But he does, in a way, answer it. After stressing that all seeds planted in the ground must "die" and are then harvested in whatever bodily form God chooses for them, he says that the animal body which has died will be succeeded by what he calls the spiritual body.

An immense amount has been written about how we are to understand the notion of the spiritual body, in Greek the *soma pneumatikon*. Those who do not wish to think that the spiritual body is a body at all lay much stress on the fact that Paul also says (v. 50) that flesh and blood can never possess the Kingdom of God. But the term Paul uses in that verse, *sarx*, is not the word for the body (*soma*). *Sarx*, or "flesh," is used by Paul as a symbol for the corrupted physical nature that we derive from Adam; this corrupted human nature cannot, indeed, inherit the Kingdom. But it does not follow from this that those who inherit the Kingdom will not have physical bodies, only that they will not have *corruptible* bodies. I think he means that the *soma pneumatikon* is not a spirit but an incorruptible body, that is, the body of a person who has been redeemed from corruption. It will, Paul says, have glory and power, and be clothed with immortality. But this does not entail that it is not spatial, three-dimensional, or material. Not only is this the most natural reading of what Paul says, but it is enshrined in the church's creeds, where believers declare that they believe in the resurrection *of the body*.

Paul's letters are occasional writings, not systematic theological treatises. So there are many questions that he does not address, or only addresses briefly and in passing. The first such question is: *who* will be raised? If the answer is that everyone will, does this mean that all are saved? And if the answer to that is no, what is to become of the others? The second question is: if the resurrection of which Paul speaks is a *future* event, what are we to expect between the time of our death and that future event? A third question is: what of those whose lives are cut off early, or who have not heard the Christian message, or who have otherwise not completed the process that leads to repentance and divine acceptance?

Paul says that as in Adam all die, so in Christ all will be made alive. It is no doubt possible to read this as implying that Christ's sacrifice, of itself, saves everyone, and there has always been a "universalist" strand in Christian thought. But it has never been more than a minority view, since it seems inconsistent with the fundamental thrust of Christian theology that each person is presented with a *choice* to accept or reject the route to salvation. So Paul is usually taken to be saying that all who are in Christ (that is, all who have accepted him) will be made alive, not that Christ makes all alive (whether they have accepted him or not). We then face this question: are those who are not destined to salvation to be raised or not?

Here there is a choice between supposing that their fate is simple extinction or holding that they are raised only to be condemned. Obviously, it is this second view that has dominated Christian history. It has taken the form of depictions of a Last Judgment in which the saved and the damned are separated and sent to opposite destinations. These destinations have been imagined in both crude and subtle ways. There is no doubt that the subtler afterlife predictions are in part attempts to avoid too great a reliance on the cosmology of the first century, when Christian expectations were first formulated. These assumed what Rudolf Bultmann has called the three-story universe, with Heaven above, earth in the middle, and Hell underneath. The drama of redemption was thought of as one in which the Son of God came down from Heaven, lived for a time on earth, was crucified and descended into Hell, and then was raised again for a time to be seen once more on earth, from which he ascended and to which he will come down again in glory at the end of time. Modern scientific understandings of the nature of the cosmos close us off forever from both the three-story universe and from the more interesting but still physically unavailable worlds that Dante and Milton describe.

It is also clear that the New Testament writers, including St. Paul, believed that Christ's return would take place soon. Hence we find Paul (in 1 Thessalonians 4) writing about how those still living would relate to Christ's Second Coming and seeking to reassure them that those who had already died would then rise. As the years went by, the expectation of the Second Coming receded and interest shifted to the interim state between death and resurrection. The pre-Christian belief that each individual would be judged at death and would then be with God or cut off from God reasserted itself. To be combined with the expectation of the final resurrection, this has to be held in a particular way: it has to be supposed that at death the person continues to exist in a bodiless or disembodied state, and that at the final resurrection each person will receive back the body that he or she left at death, or, of course, another. If there is a judgment of each person at death, then the emerging expectation is of two judgments: an individual one at death, to be followed by a universal judgment, or judgment of the nations, at the close of history. This is a somewhat uncomfortable combination, since there would seem to be no room for these two judgments to give different verdicts for the same individual, so one or the other becomes something of a formality. It is not surprising, then, that many Christians have thought that at death one is immediately destined to Heaven or to Hell with no intermediate state, and presumably no body.

One feature of all these expectations is fundamental. Whether the dead are to go to their final destinations at once or only after an interim time, what determines their final destination is whether they have availed themselves of the sacrifice of Christ during this life. Nor does there seem to be any place in Christian expectations for the notion of a decisive spiritual reorientation *after* death.

There are two ways in which this last statement has to be modified. First, there is a longstanding attempt to address the question of the fate of those who died before the coming of Christ. The First Letter of Peter says that Christ "made his proclamation to the imprisoned spirits" (1 Pt 3:19). The tradition deriving from this text holds that between his death and resurrection Christ descended and preached to those who had died before his coming. A second teaching that represents a modification of the claim that each person's fate is decided by the time of death is the Catholic doctrine of purgatory. According to this, those in the interim state who have not, prior to death, committed sins for which there is no redemption, but who are guilty of offenses for which they have not done adequate penance before death, suffer a period of purgation or redemptive suffering. It is important to bear in mind that this doctrine presupposes a double judgment, in that the trials of purgatory are intended only for those whose sins are deemed to be forgivable and destined to be forgiven. It does not represent any fundamental modification of the belief that redemption or condemnation are essentially determined by the time of death. It is still rejected by Protestants, though it has been part of both the Catholic and Orthodox traditions.

What Is Essential in Christian Belief about the Afterlife?

First, I think it is essential for the Christian to believe that there *is* an afterlife. From time to time, thinkers who consider themselves Christians argue that the faith does not require this belief, or even that it is not consistent with its demands.[3] Such views require us to interpret Christian claims about salvation as claims about the transformation of the personality in this life. But the transformation that Christians claim their new life involves is not something that can be observed here and now in its entirety. It always has a large promissory note attached. Such improvement as can be discerned in the "saved" personality is seen as a part of a process that will not be exhausted here and now. If this promise of continuing change were not to be realized—if there were no hereafter—all the Christian language about salvation, eternal life, cleansing, and the rest would be utopian and false. But if it is true, then the afterlife is a necessity, not just a doctrinal bonus.

But it does not follow from this that someone who accepts these Christian claims must also accept any particular understanding of what sort of afterlife awaits us. There are two features of the original Christian proclamation that, it seems clear to me, we are not now in a position to accept. The first is the belief in what Bultmann calls the three-story universe. Even the least scientifically sophisticated of us now knows that the earth we live on is not sandwiched between a Heaven that is up above and a netherworld that is below and entered through the grave. This, of course, does not prove there is no Heaven or Hell or other abode of spirits, but it does prove that if there are such realms, they are not to be understood as literally above and below us. It follows from this that Luke's story of a physical ascension cannot be literally true.

Something else in the primitive Christian proclamation must also be abandoned. We know that the earth we live on is immeasurably older than Christians used to think, and that our species is a latecomer that appeared on the scene after many other species had developed—and after many of our predecessors had lost out in the battle for survival. However the process of evolution is understood in detail, one fact about it is clear to everyone: the survival of the fittest is a process that requires the disappearance of the less fit. This tells us something fundamental about the natural world of which we are a part: the creative processes that have led to all the forms of life that we now know are processes in which death is not an alien aberration, introduced through human wickedness, but an integral and indispensable means of selection. Paul is wrong to say that mortality, per se, came into the world through Adam. This does not mean that Christ does not, or did not, conquer death in some vitally important sense; but it does mean that death, in and of itself, cannot be read by Christians as a curse.

I also think Christians can disagree, as scholars do, on the reliability of the post-resurrection appearance narratives in the four gospels. These narratives seem to be later in composition than Paul's statements about Jesus' appearances, with which they do not conform very closely; nor are they obviously consistent with one another. Just as it is not so radical to question whether Christians have to accept all the details of the accounts of Jesus' birth in Matthew and Luke, so it seems to me quite possible for

Christians to question many of the details of the post-resurrection narratives, such as the angels at the tomb.[4]

This leads to a further and more substantial point of debate. If we compare what Paul says in 1 Corinthians 15 with the gospel narratives of the appearances, especially that in Luke, we are struck by the fact that while Paul uses wholly visual language to talk of these appearances, stressing over and over that Christ was *seen* by those whom he lists, the gospel accounts give much more emphasis to the tangible and three-dimensional character of Jesus' presence, telling us that he ate with his disciples, that the women clutched his feet, and that Thomas was told to touch his hands and side. It is almost as though some of these details are stressed in order to remind us of the *physicality* of the resurrection.

If Christians can legitimately debate the reliability of these gospel narratives, I think it is also legitimate for them to debate how far the resurrection of Jesus—and the future resurrection to which his followers look forward—must be understood in physical terms. Just as there is debate about the way we are to read the accounts of Jesus' resurrection, so there is debate about how we should read what Paul predicts will happen at the time of the resurrection of the dead. Is the *soma pneumatikon* really a *body*? Paul Gooch thinks not, in opposition to Oscar Cullmann and others who are convinced Paul does mean this.[5] I have to say that the physical reading seems to me the more natural reading of what he says, and this in turn suggests that what he also says about Jesus' appearances should not be read in a way that undermines the gospel narratives in this respect, however hard it may be to square with them in other ways.

I pass on to one other serious area where there have always been differing opinions among Christians, namely, the problem of the interim state of the dead. What is the condition of those who have died but not yet risen? Paul refers to them as sleeping and also speaks of his own longing to be with God at once and not stay here in this world. As the anticipation of a general resurrection in the near future has receded, it has been common for many to suppose that the transition to blessedness or perdition is immediate and that Paul's teaching is best interpreted as referring symbolically to a redemption and judgment that is individual and not general. While it seems clear to me which way it is natural to read the texts, and that only one way of reading seems to fit *all* the texts, these are still matters on which disagreement seems to me to be quite in order.

PHILOSOPHICAL DIFFICULTIES IN THE CHRISTIAN VIEW

Philosophical difficulties in the Christian view are very great. I can only indicate briefly what they are and how far the Christian claims about the hereafter can be defended against them.[6]

If you ask unbelievers why they think that belief in an afterlife has to be rejected, they are most likely to emphasize the fact that mental abilities and conscious thought and feeling depend upon the brain and nervous system. One response to this that tempts some Christians, myself included, is the following. The basic Christian teaching about life after death is the doctrine of resurrection. This tells us that we shall live after death *in a body*. So it does not matter that science and common experience show us how much our mental lives depend on our bodily condition.

Christians who argue this way usually go on to say that the belief that is inconsistent with the physical basis of personality is not the belief in resurrection but the quite different belief in the immortality of an immaterial soul. This belief is given its first clear and authoritative expression not in the Hebrew or Christian scriptures, but in Plato's dialogue, the *Phaedo*. The Platonic view of human personality is indeed hard to square with the conviction that human personality arises from physical and biological sources and is impossible without them. But Christians, the argument goes, do not need to be concerned with that, because this is not the view of humanity they find in their scriptures.[7]

If we accept this argument and say no more, then we have to admit certain consequences. There are, in the first place, significant implications concerning the interim state between death and resurrection. If we think that there can be no human personality without a basis in a physical organism, then we have to conclude that there is no interim state at all, that the dead cease to be until they are literally re-created or reconstituted on the Last Day. An alternative to this is to suggest that we will continue, but in an immediate resurrection-body that we inherit at once, even while the former earthly body lies in the ground. Whatever the merits of these suggestions, they force us to disregard a large number of the secondary texts.

There is a further difficulty. It is one that many Christian thinkers have ignored, and which, when raised, is quite often dismissed as frivolous. I do not think it is frivolous. If in the future each of us, or each of the saved, is to appear in a body that comes into being by special act of God, and may well be more glorious than the corrupted and diseased body that died, how can we say that these future persons will be *ourselves*? Surely what will succeed each of us will merely be a replica or duplicate, and not we ourselves at all.

To some this seems like a piece of foolish logic-chopping; but that sort of reaction does not make the issue go away. There is, of course, an obvious way out. It is to say that something exists in between death and resurrection that preserves our identity at the time of the resurrection, and that this is the soul or spirit. The soul continues after death and gets back its body—or another, transformed body—at the last, but it is the soul that preserves our identity in between. One can hold this without supposing, as Plato did, that disembodied existence is our natural state. It is merely the state in which we persist when this phase of life is over.

This view fits well enough with all the texts and seems to answer the replica difficulty. But it does have some problems of its own. In the first place, do we understand what it would be like to persist in being without a body? A disembodied person could not do any of the things that one has to have a body to do. So a disembodied person could not walk, run, sit, talk, sing, smile, laugh, cry, wave, or shake hands. It follows immediately from this that disembodied beings would not be visible or touchable or audible. So they could not, it seems, meet one another, let alone communicate with us. Many people who believe in life after death think they believe in the separation of the soul from the body. But in practice they go on ascribing physical characteristics to the souls of survivors in a way that is quite inconsistent with saying they have no bodies.

But the real problem with bodiless spirit existence is that it does not clearly provide for identity after death. Many philosophers have pointed out that our understanding of a person's identity through time is intimately connected with that person's physical continuity. Our mental life changes with great rapidity. Yet we ascribe all these changing mental events to the same person. If we ask what justifies us in doing this, the obvious answer is that they are all connected with the same physical organism. It, too, changes over the years, but it does so more slowly; it is continuous through time in a way that our mental life is not. So there seems to be a difficulty about the identity of incorporeal or disembodied beings: how can we provide in our thinking for their identity through time?

I think that these philosophical difficulties are grave ones, and that they make it hard to resort to the belief in a bodiless spirit as the bearer of personal identity after death. I am more inclined to confront the problem of replication and to defend the doctrine of resurrection in its starkest form, than to try to mix it in with the belief in disembodied spirits.

It is true, though, that this combination seems to be necessary if we wish to retain the content and implications of all the biblical texts that teach us about the afterlife.[8] And *this* fact brings us up against the huge question of how far Christians are required to hold onto the details of all the biblical texts. It is not surprising that we end here, but I have to leave this issue unexplored.

Notes

[1] See, for example, Godfrey Vesey, ed., *The Philosophy in Christianity* (Cambridge: Cambridge University Press, 1989).

[2] Quotations from the New Testament are from the *New English Bible* (Oxford and Cambridge University Presses, 1961).

[3] For an interesting recent example, see D. Z. Phillips, *Death and Immortality* (London: Macmillan, 1970).

[4] See Raymond E. Brown, *The Virginal Conception and Bodily Resurrection of Jesus* (London: Geoffrey Chapman, 1974).

[5] Paul W. Gooch, *Partial Knowledge* (Notre Dame, Ind.: University of Notre Dame Press, 1987), chap. 3; Oscar Cullmann, *Immortality of the Soul or Resurrection of the Dead?* (London: Epworth Press, 1958).

[6] The fullest statement of the case against all forms of belief in an afterlife is to be found in Antony Flew, *The Logic of Mortality* (Oxford: Blackwell, 1987). For a recent Christian defense, see Stephen T. Davis, *Risen Indeed* (Grand Rapids, Mich.: Eerdmans, 1993).

[7] For the implications of this contrast, see particularly Cullmann.

[8] I have been convinced of this, reluctantly, by the arguments of John W. Cooper, *Body, Soul, and Life Everlasting* (Grand Rapids, Mich.: Eerdmans, 1989).

3

Islam

Hanna Kassis

Every soul shall taste of death; you shall surely be paid in full your wages on the Day of Resurrection. Whosoever is removed from the Fire and admitted to Paradise, shall win the triumph. The present life is but the joy of delusion (Qur'ān, 3:185).

"ONLY HE REMAINS"

My introduction, as a non-Muslim, to the fundamentals of Islam was in the context of a funeral. I must have been somewhere between seven and nine years of age when, in the company of my father, I joined a throng of mourners along the main street that traversed the city of Gaza, in Palestine. Someone important, as far as the community was concerned, had died. I know neither the identity of the deceased nor the circumstances of his death. I was aware that the deceased was Muslim because his funeral passed through the mosque rather than a church. There was, I recall, a hushed silence among the crowd of men and children who lined the street as the cortege moved from the mosque to the cemetery, and an atmosphere of awe and affection prevailed. But far more effective was the sound in the background. In a display of ecumenicity (long before the term acquired currency), the pealing church bells were ringing in clusters of three tolls, alternating with a chanted cry from the minaret of an adjacent mosque, *subḥānahu al-wāḥid ul-ḥayy ud-dā'im ulladhī lā yamūt* ("Praise be to Him, the One, the Ever-living, the Eternal, who never dies"). As the cortege passed, my father waved his hand, as did others, and tearfully echoed, borrowing from Islam, *huwa al-bāqī* ("Only He remains"). In this moment of grief, the emphasis was less on the deceased and more on "the One who never dies"; the personal yielded to the eternal.

A discussion of any institution in Islam must begin with a restatement of the fundamentals of the faith as these pertain to our subject. God (Allāh) alone is God, there is none other; all that is seen and unseen is God's creation, and all that is created shall perish. Death (*mawt*)[1] is not a punishment but a natural termination of life. God alone is everlasting, and it is God who ordains both death and life.

While, as in the case of every religious tradition, Islam retained traces of some older beliefs and practices pertaining to death and burial, its view of life, death, and the afterlife marks a total break from that of the pre-Islamic past. In the age that preceded Islam in the Arabian Peninsula (the birthplace of Islam), an age known as the *jāhilīyah* ("the age of ignorance"), the cosmos was seen as comprising two distinct constituents. The first was the inanimate physical world, which was not subject to the vicissitudes of time or aging and was thus perceived as permanent and imperishable. By contrast, the second constituent, that of the animate world, was perishable. Breath and blood were seen as the vital elements that activated the animate world. Death came as a result of the cessation of one or another of these vital elements. Cessation of breath was the means to a natural death; death as a result of the shedding of blood was unnatural and required retribution, without which the soul of the dead wandered restlessly in the desert until avenged.

As in other societies of the Near East, biblical as well as prebiblical, the burial of the dead was an important religious ritual for pre-Islamic Arabs. It marked the passage from one form of existence to another, from the land of the living to the abyss of the dead. Not unlike the case of unavenged death by murder, failure to bury the corpse of the dead deprived the soul of its eternal rest. As a result, an elaborate ritual surrounded the burial of the dead. Paramount in these circumstances was not so much the significance of the individual but the honor of the tribe to which the deceased belonged. In the case of unavenged murder, the honor of the tribe was tarnished until vengeance was achieved; in the case of failure to bury the dead, only fulfillment of burial requirements would restore tribal honor. Upholding the honor of the tribe was far more important than the preservation of the life of the individual.

Islam radically changed these conceptions. Both the animate (pertaining to humans and animals) and the inanimate (physical) worlds are subject to God's decree. According to Islam, the apparent permanence of the physical world was a fallacy that yielded to the certainty of the impermanence of all things and beings. In language that overturned the earlier hypotheses regarding the physical world, the Qur'ān unequivocally states, "Thou seest the mountains and thinkest them firmly fixed; but they shall pass away as the clouds pass away."[2] In one of the more lyrical chapters of the Qur'ān the same idea is presented with the affirmation that only God is permanent: "All that dwells upon the earth is perishing, yet still abides the Face of thy Lord, majestic, splendid."[3]

At the level of the ideal, the tribe was replaced by the *ummah*, the universal community of faith. The individual came to be seen as a unique creation of God, owing ultimate loyalty and submission only to God. Life itself proceeded from God, not from the loins of the fathers or the wombs of the mothers, which are only the instruments of God's creative act. Consequently, the individual belonged to God, not to the tribe as had been hitherto believed, and the brotherhood or sisterhood of the *ummah* was far more important than tribal (or national) affiliation. And as a gift from God, the life of that individual became sacred, protected by God's Law. Its purpose is to please God (*marḍāt Allāh*) and to find peace with God, not to satisfy the needs of the tribe. A Muslim is deeply moved when reciting the verse from the Qur'ān, "Say, 'My prayer, my ritual sacrifice, my living, my dying—all belong to God, the Lord of all Being.'"[4] Therefore, the primary purpose of life is to walk in the path of God, to abide by God's ordinances, and to secure God's pleasure. This contrasts with the pre-Islamic view that life's purpose was to ensure the honor of the tribe and the survival of the group.

Similarly, death was no longer seen as the result of the disruptive action of time and age. Instead, Muslim belief holds that it is God—and God alone—who defines the life span of every living thing and brings each life to its completion at the time determined by God alone. Not unlike Judaism and Christianity, Islam teaches that it is God who gives and it is God who takes away. According to a Tradition preserved by al-Bukhārī,[5] when one of his daughters lost her son, the Prophet consoled her and counseled forbearance, saying that "God has taken what belongs to Him as He had given of what is His; everything occurs in accordance with His appointed term." This Tradition is in harmony with the teaching of the Qur'ān that says, "Yet give thou good tidings unto the patient [ones] who, when they are visited by an affliction, say, 'Surely we belong to God, and to Him we return.'"[6]

The belief that God determines the time of the expiry of one's life on earth is reflected in such vocabulary associated with death as the noun *wafāt* (literally, "fulfillment, accomplishment"), the verb (in the passive voice) *tuwuffiya* ("One has been brought to accomplishment"), or the complete statement *tawaffāhu Allāh* ("God has brought the term of one's life to its fulfillment"). Such accomplishment or fulfillment hastens one's meeting with God in the hope of receiving God's blessing and meriting admission to Paradise.

For the pre-Islamic Arabs, death was a realm into which one passed and dwelled at the end of one's life on earth; it was a state of inanimate torpor as opposed to the animation of life. By contrast, for Islam, rather than being the end of life, death is but a passageway from earthly life (*al-ḥayāt al-dunyā*, "the lower life"), which is transient (*dār al-fanā'*, "the abode of perishability"), to the Hereafter (*al-ākhirah*), wherein is eternal life (*dār al-baqā'*, "the abode of permanence"). And while for pre-Islamic Arabs the realms of life and death were governed by different deities,[7] according to Islam, God alone is the sovereign of both realms.

"HERE I AM LORD": PREPARATION AND BURIAL OF THE DEAD

Although the Qur'ān has nothing to say about funerals, Muslim scholarship turned to the Traditions for guidance, arriving at minute guidelines for the details of the burial of the dead. The task of formulating these details fell to a genre of scholarship known as *fiqh* (religious jurisprudence). The formulations arrived at by the scholars, or jurisconsults (*fuqahā'*, plural of *faqīh*), depended not only on the creativity of the scholar himself but also on the sectarian (*sunnī* and *shī'ah*)[8] and jurisprudential group to which he belonged.[9]

It would be impractical to attempt to summarize here the various funerary details prescribed by the different schools of jurisprudence in Islam. Therefore, only the most common practices will be outlined. It is of paramount importance to remember that these practices were not so much social conventions as they were religious rituals. This is best evident from the first requirement, which is the act of reminding the dying person of the primary statement of faith, the *shahādah* or the testimony that there is no deity other than God (Allāh) and that Muḥammad is God's Prophet and Messenger. The invocation of the Divine Name is the first thing a Muslim hears at the moment of birth; it is the last utterance to be said or heard at the final moment of a person's life on earth. The family, therefore, turns the face of the dying person toward the Ka'ba, in Mecca,[10] and whispers the *shahādah* in his or her ear. The dead person is then placed on a stretcher with the head in the direction of Mecca. It is as if dying is an act of prayer with the rituals of prayer being applied.

Those present at the moment of death should implore God to make the dying person's passage easy and without pain. Death is followed by the ritual of *ghusl* or the washing of the body of the deceased. This ritual also begins with the invocation of the Name of God, the Merciful, the Compassionate. The practice of *ghusl* appears to date back to the time when the Prophet ordered that the body of his dead daughter be washed several times (always an odd number). According to a Tradition narrated by Umm 'Aṭīyah, a woman who had traveled from Iraq to Medinah to visit her son, "The Apostle of God came to us as we were washing the body of his deceased daughter and said, 'Wash her with water and [the leaves of] the lote-tree (*sidr*)[11] three, five or more times, if you deem it necessary, and steep leaves of camphor in the water at the end.'. . .We informed him when we were finished and he gave us his waist-cloth and ordered us to wrap her in it." Following another Tradition, "It was also said that they were to start with the right side and with the parts of the body that were washed in ablution." According to yet another Tradition narrated by Abū 'Abbas (one among the trustworthy sources of narration of Tradition) and referring to another dead person, the Prophet ordered, "Wash him with water and [the leaves of] the lote-tree and wrap him in two shrouds; do not place perfume on him nor dye his hair; he should be prepared to appear on the Day of Resurrection ready to say the *talbiyah*, (saying, 'Here I am, Lord')." Yet another Tradition, deemed weak in its transmission, gives the reason behind the ritual, saying that "Upon his death, the angels washed Adam with water and [the leaves of] the lote-tree; they prepared a tomb and buried him in it saying, 'This shall be your rule regarding your dead, Children of Adam (Humankind).'"

The details of the ritual of *ghusl* (washing the body) are dealt with minutely by the jurisconsults (*fuqahā'*). Some examples: the body is not stripped entirely at the time of washing; bathing must be performed by persons of the same sex; in cases where disease may make it unhygienic, bathing is replaced by pouring water over the body.

After being washed, the body is wrapped in shrouds made of simple cloth, preferably white, in preparation for a hurried burial. A Tradition says, "Make haste to bury the dead person. If he (or she) has done well, you would be doing him (or her) well to hurry him (or her) to God; and if he (or she) had done otherwise, it would be an evil of which you rid yourselves quickly." Therefore, burial takes place before night descends on the day of death or, if late, the following day.

Covered completely, the body is carried on an open bier to the cemetery. It is considered a meritorious act to share in carrying a bier. A stop at the mosque may be made, though it is not required. Otherwise, the procession continues to the cemetery without stopping. A Tradition says, "If you walk in a funeral procession, do not sit down until the burial is completed." To avoid ritual lamentation (striking the face or tearing the hair) and open emotion, women are not permitted to follow a funeral.

Prayers are said at the tomb only after the settlement of all debts owed by the deceased. A close relative officiates, standing by the head of a male deceased or by the trunk of a female deceased. No prayers are said over the tomb of an unbeliever or a person who committed suicide; they are not required over a martyr or a stillborn infant ("a baby who did not cry"). After the sincere intention (*niyyah*) is pronounced, the glorification of God (*takbīr*, saying *Allāhu akbar*, "God is great") is proclaimed four times, with hands raised. The first of these proclamations is followed by the recitation of the opening chapter (*Fātiḥah*) of the Qur'ān, the second by a recitation of the praises of the Prophet, the third by a supplication for the deceased, and the last by a supplication for those attending the funeral. The funeral ritual is then concluded with the recitation of the invocation of peace upon the Prophet, his household, and all believers (*taslīm*), which is said twice.

The burial takes place immediately after the prayer and without a coffin. The grave must be deep and may be either in the form of a deep hole or a trench facing Mecca. An odd number of the nearest relatives descend into the grave to fit the body in. The clothes are loosened, the face is turned toward Mecca, and the *shahādah* is whispered once more in the ear of the deceased. When this has been done, earth is placed loosely over the body and three handfuls are sprinkled on the grave by those in attendance, who should individually say a prayer for the forgiveness of the sins of the deceased.

"TASTING THE NEARER CHASTISEMENT": JUDGMENT IN THE TOMB

The belief developed that judgment begins in the tomb soon after death. Accordingly, the deceased is visited by two angels, Munkar and Nakīr, who make the dead person sit up in the grave in order to answer questions of faith. (The dirt was placed loosely over the body, in order to enable the dead person to sit up when the time of questioning comes.) If, when questioned about the testimony of faith—the uniqueness of God and the identity of Muḥammad—the deceased answers correctly and unwaveringly, he or she is left alone until the Resurrection of the Dead and the Day of Judgment. If, on the other hand, he or she is a disbeliever who answers incorrectly, the angels Munkar and Nakīr [citing the Qur'ān] "shall spread their hands [saying], 'Give up your souls; today shall you be recompensed with an ignominous chastisement because you spoke against God other than the truth'" (Qur'ān 6:93). Having caused them to die, the angels "will smite their faces and their backs [saying], 'Taste the punishment of burning'" (Qur'ān 8:50). This punishment is known as *'adhāb al-qabr* ("torment in the tomb").

While such a concept has no evident mention in the Qur'ān, the *fuqahā'* found support for the notion in the interpretation of certain verses, as has been pointed out. Support for the notion of a twofold chastisement, the first of which is in the tomb, was found in the passage, "We [God is speaking] will chastise them twice, then they shall be turned back to a grievous chastisement" (Qur'ān 9:101), as well as in the passage, "And most certainly We [God is speaking] will make them taste of the nearer chastisement before the greater chastisement that haply they may turn" (Qur'ān 32:21).

Soon after death, some would regret their failure to accomplish what God had demanded of them in this life and would ask to return to earth to do the good they had left undone. But they will be prevented from doing so by a barrier (*barzakh*) that will bar their path until the Day of the Resurrection:

> Till, when death comes to one of them, he says, "My Lord, return me; haply I shall do righteousness in that I forsook." Nay, it is but a word he speaks; and there, behind them, is a barrier until the day that they shall be raised up (Qur'ān, 23:99-101).

"WHEN SHALL BE THE DAY OF RESURRECTIONS?"

While the notion of chastisement in the tomb has been developed by the scientists of religion, the belief in a Day of Resurrection and a Day of Judgment finds support in the Qur'ān. As certain as is the proclamation of the uniqueness of God and of God's sovereignty, likewise certain is the affirmation of the Hereafter (*al-ḥayāt al-'ākhirah*). It is equally strong an article of faith that there is a Day of Resurrection (*yawm al-qiyāma*) and of Judgment (*yawm al-dīn*) on which the living and the dead shall answer for their thoughts and actions; that Paradise (*al-janna*) is the reward of those who abide by God's Law, and that Hell (*jahannam*) is the penalty for those who rebel against it. Again and again, the Qur'ān restates the contrast of this life (*al- ḥayāt al-dunyā*) with the life to come (*al-ḥayāt al-'ākhira*). And while without any doubt this life is a gift of God to be enjoyed in accordance with God's Law, it remains nothing more than a prelude of limited duration to the life to come; "Say, 'The enjoyment of this world is little; the world to come is better for him who fears God'" (Qur'ān, 4:77).

The chapter (sūrah) in the Qur'ān entitled "The Resurrection" (Qur'ān, 75) begins with the affirmation of the Day of Resurrection, "No! I swear by the Day of Resurrection," and evokes, in powerful rhapsodic fashion, the portents of the Day of Resurrection:

> Nay, but man desires to continue on as a
> libertine,
> asking, "When shall be the Day of
> Resurrection?"
> But when the sight is dazed
> and the moon is eclipsed,
> and the sun and moon are brought together,
> upon that day man shall say, "Whither to flee?"
> No indeed; not a refuge!
> Upon that day the recourse shall be to thy Lord.
> Upon that day man shall be told his former
> deeds and his latter;
> nay, man shall be a clear proof against himself,
> even though he offer his excuses.
>
> (Qur'ān, 75:5-15)

The Qur'ān emphasizes that the time (*al-sā'ah*, "the Hour") at which life on earth will end, ushering in the Resurrection, is known only to God. "The people will question thee [Muḥammad] concerning the Hour. Say, 'The knowledge of it is only with God'" (Qur'ān, 33:63).

That it will come to pass is certain in spite of the fact that most people do not believe it (Qur'ān, 40:59). When the Hour comes, it will be signalled by terrifying portents: "The Hour has drawn nigh: the moon is split" (Qur'ān, 54:1), or, "Surely the earthquake of the Hour is a mighty thing; on the day when you behold it, every suckling woman shall neglect the child she has suckled, and every pregnant woman shall deposit her burden, and thou shalt see mankind drunk, yet they are not drunk, but God's chastisement is terrible" (Qur'ān, 22:1-2).

As in the case of its predecessor and sister-religion, Christianity, the image of the Hour captured the imagination of the believer, yielding varied illustrations that portray its imminence. The Traditions are replete with portents of the Hour: the sun will rise in the west, fire will consume the earth from east to west, the quaking earth will swallow up many tribes and nations, and so on.

These and many similar images of the signs of the Hour are but an illustration of the creative imagination of the believer, elaborating on the otherwise concise and evocative signals mentioned in the Qur'ān. As a result, and perhaps borrowing from Christian and Jewish eschatology, a vivid eschatological picture of the end of earthly life was developed in Muslim religious thought. One of the most detailed is that of the anti-Christ (*al-Dajjāl*, "the false one") and the return of Jesus, son of Mary.[12] According to this eschatology, the anti-Christ, a manifestation of Satan or one of his allies, shall appear. The Muslims shall be lured away by Satan from the fulfillment of their divinely ordained obligations. Great tribulation will precede his appearance and he will have provisions to satisfy people's needs and entice them to follow him. This will be facilitated by his resemblance to Christ. Thus, believing that he is the returned Messiah, many shall be led astray and he shall have dominion over the entire world, except for Mecca and Medina, for forty years. His dominion will be checked by Jesus, the Messiah, who will return (even with a spear in his hand) and will fight the anti-Christ and destroy him. The cosmic battle will take place in Palestine (or Syria), after which Jesus will restore faith, justice, and peace—a golden age that shall precede the Day of Resurrection.[13]

The Messianic victory over the anti-Christ will be followed by the sounding of a blast, or two blasts, of the Trumpet. The Qur'ān makes several references to this eschatological event, around which a lively picture of the Last Day has developed.[14] Following the first blast and in preparation for the Resurrection, all living things will die. An interval will precede the sounding of the second blast of the Trumpet, at which all the dead will be brought back to life and assembled in preparation for the Judgment.

The Qur'ān and the traditions that developed from its interpretation give us a picture of the Day of Judgment as vivid and varied as the carvings on the tympanums of many medieval churches. As judgment is individual, rather than by groups, every person will stand before God on that day to answer for his or her actions. "If thou couldst see when they are stationed before their Lord! He will say, 'Is not this the truth?' They will say, 'Yes indeed, by our Lord!' He will say, 'Then taste the chastisement for your unbelief'" (Qur'ān, 6:30). Each person will carry a record of his or her deeds, the righteous in their right hand,[15] while the wicked will carry it in their left hand or behind their back.[16] On that day, the Day of Reckoning (*yawm al-ḥisāb*), God will ask each to read his or her record,

> And We shall bring forth for him [every person], on the Day of Resurrection, a book he shall find spread wide open. "Read thy book! Thy soul suffices thee this day as a reckoner against thee" (Qur'ān, 17:13-14).

Whereupon, the wicked will wish that they could be spared the encounter,

> But as for him who is given his book in his left hand [the wicked], he shall say, "Would that I had not been given my book and not known my reckoning!" (Qur'ān, 69:25-26).

On that day, they shall render account (*ḥisāb*) of their actions individually, and those about whom there is any doubt shall be weighed in the cosmic scales.

> Then he whose scales are heavy—they are the prosperers, and he whose scales are light—they have lost their souls in Gehenna dwelling forever, the Fire smiting their faces the while they glower there (Qur'ān, 23:102-4).

Those found to be sinners will not benefit from intercession, for none shall intercede except by God's authority. Tradition has allowed for intercession by "those who bear the Throne of God" and by Muḥammad on the strength of the Qur'anic passage, "it may be that thy Lord will raise thee up to a laudable station" (Qur'ān 17:79). On the strength of the interpretation of some passages from the Qur'ān, further tradition speaks of intercession by angels, Apostles, Prophets, martyrs, and saintly ones (*awliyā'*). One such passage says,

> But they are honoured servants that outstrip Him not in speech, and perform as He commands. He knows what is before them and behind them, and they intercede not save for him with whom He is well-pleased, and they tremble in awe of Him (Qur'ān, 21:26-28).

God may intercede on behalf of those who genuinely repent and seek forgiveness. However, intercession will not apply to any who have associated another god with God.

Tradition alone preserves an image of a basin (*ḥawḍ*) at which Muḥammad will assemble his community in the hope for admission to Paradise. The poor and those who were denied the comforts of the earthly life shall be in the first ranks.

When he pleads with God for his community, Muḥammad will be told that he does not know what they had done following his death.

"UNTO THE PATH OF HELL"

Failing to receive intercession, the wicked shall be marched along the "Path of Hell" (*ṣirāṭ al-jaḥīm*), to the burning Fire:

> Muster those who did evil, their wives, and that they were serving, apart from God, and guide them unto the path of Hell! (Qur'ān, 37:22-23).

Hell (*jahannam*) is frequently mentioned in the Qur'ān, and occasionally described. One passage gave later tradition the impression of Hell being transportable,

> When the earth is ground to powder, and thy Lord comes, and the angels rank on rank, and Gehenna is brought out, upon that day man will remember; and how shall the Reminder be for him? (Qur'ān, 89:21-23).

The Qur'ān depicts Hell as a burning fire which "whensoever it abates We shall increase for them the Blaze" (Qur'ān 17:97). It burns with such fury that it nearly bursts. The sinners "shall go round between it and between hot, boiling water" (Qur'ān, 55:44), regretting their failure to heed the warning given them,

> When they are cast into it they will hear it sighing, the while it boils and wellnigh bursts asunder with rage. As often as a troop is cast into it, its keepers ask them, "Came there no warner to you?" They say, "Yes indeed, a warner came to us; but we cried lies, saying, 'God has not sent down anything; you are only in great error.'" They also say, "If we had only heard, or had understood, we would not have been of the inhabitants of the Blaze" (Qur'ān, 67:7-10).

"ENTER THOU MY PARADISE"

As for those who are righteous or those who repented and whose sins God has forgiven, they shall gain admission to Paradise, which is mentioned in the Qur'ān more frequently than Hell. Paradise is very vividly described in the Qur'ān in a manner that has been frequently misunderstood or intentionally misrepresented in the West. Chapter 55, *al-raḥmān* ("The All-Merciful") offers an image that may best be appreciated symbolically and against the backdrop of the social history of seventh-century Arabia. The chapter is hymnic in nature and contains an often repeated chorus, "O which of your Lord's bounties will you and you deny?" The earlier part of the chapter is akin to a hymn of praise to God for creation. This is followed by the reminder that "all that dwells upon the earth is perishing, yet still abides the Face of thy Lord, majestic, splendid" (Qur'ān 55:26-27).

Then, following the brief depiction of Hell, there is a resplendent image of Paradise, which is depicted as

> two Gardens, abounding in branches—therein two fountains of running water—therein of every fruit two kinds—reclining upon couches lined with brocade, the fruits of the gardens nigh to gather—therein maidens restraining their glances, untouched before them by any man or jinn—lovely as rubies, beautiful as coral. Shall the recompense of goodness be other than goodness? (Qur'ān, 55:48-60).[17]

Taken at face value, as regrettably has often been the case, the powerful and evocative symbolism can be readily distorted. What must be sought, instead, is the impact of the total picture of the mercy and compassion of God bestowed upon the faithful, a picture not unlike the *locus amoenus*, the location of pleasance, the garden motif borrowed by Christian poets to depict Paradise.[18]

It is correctly said that one statement or image of scripture is best understood through another image or statement from elsewhere in the same scripture. The Qur'anic image of the pleasance of the Afterlife for those upon whom God bestows it may best be placed in clear focus by another passage that says,

> O soul at peace,
> return unto thy Lord, well-pleased, well-
> pleasing!
> Enter thou among My servants!
> Enter thou My Paradise!
>
> (Qur'ān, 89:27-30)

Notes

[1] Although Arabic-speaking Muslims form but a small minority of the world Muslim community of faith (*ummah*), the primary language of Islam is Arabic. This is simply due to the fact that the Qur'ān, the revealed Word of God in Islam, was received in Arabic. Not infrequently, therefore, technical religious terminology appears in Arabic. In this context, it should be mentioned that other terms for "death" beside *mawt* exist. But with one exception, which shall be discussed below, these are not pressingly relevant to our discussion.

[2] It is an undebatable article of faith for Muslims that the Qur'ān is the non-created Word of God revealed to the Prophet Muḥammad as a guidance to humanity. As such, it is the font from which all Muslim beliefs must be primarily derived. The passage cited is an English interpretation of Chapter (*sūra*) 27, verse (*āyah*) 88; see *The Holy Qur'ān: Text, Translation and Commentary* by Abdullah Yusuf Ali.

[3] Chapter 55, verse 26, as interpreted by Arthur John Arberry, *The Koran* (Oxford University Press). I shall use Arberry's interpretation unless otherwise indicated.

[4] Chapter 6, verse 162.

[5] The Traditions (*Ḥadīth*) of the Prophet are sayings or actions of the Prophet as these are recollected by the community of faith. Assembling the Traditions constitutes a science. The substance of each Tradition (*matn*) is preceded by the names of those who had received and transmitted it (*isnād*), ultimately reaching back to the first source of the cited narration. Each link in the chain of transmission has undergone (and continues to undergo) the close scrutiny of religious scholars who are not necessarily in agreement as to what constitutes an authentic and reliable Tradition. Among several collections, that of al-Bukhārī has been widely held in high esteem.

[6] Chapter 2, verse 156 in Arberry's interpretation. The passage, *innā lillāh wa-innā ilayhi rāji'ūn* ("Surely we belong to God and to Him we return") is very frequently used to announce someone's death.

[7] In the absence of sufficient information from pre-Islamic Arabia, we are compelled to draw upon the practices and beliefs of other non-monotheistic societies of the Near East for our conclusions in this regard.

[8] The Shī'ah adhere to the unwavering belief that, according to the Qur'ān and the expressed wishes of the Prophet, sacred and temporal authority were vested in 'Alī, the cousin of the Prophet and the husband of his daughter Fāṭima, and in his designated descendants. There are primarily three groups of Shī'ah: a) The "Twelvers" (primarily in Iran), who await the return of the Imām from his occultation; b) The "Seveners" (Ismailis), who are guided by their living Imām (the Agha Khan); they are concentrated mainly in India, Pakistan, East Africa, Britain, and North America; c) The "Zaidis," who acknowledged Zaid ibn 'Alī ibn Ḥussain as the succeeding Imām.

The Sunnīs, the dominant group of Muslims, argued that authority was entrusted by the Prophet to the community of faith as a whole. They called for a continuation of "republican" rule, guided by the Qur'ān and the teachings and practices of Muḥammad (the sunna of God and God's Apostle). While victory was won by the Sunnīs, their cause was subsequently changed by the prevailing political circumstances. Instead of an elected leadership, a dynastic rule came to dominate Islamic history and the Muslim state. The Caliph (the dynastic successor of the Prophet) had to be of *ahl al-bayt* ("the household of the Prophet"), which was interpreted as being one of the tribe of Quraysh, the tribe to which the Prophet belonged. The Classical "caliphate" was destroyed in 1258 C.E. by the Mongol invasion. One form of its continuation was ended with the collapse of the Ottoman Empire in 1917.

[9] Four major schools of jurisprudence (*fiqh*) emerged among the Sunnīs and came to dominate the Islamic world. The primary concern of the scholars around whom the schools were formed was to define the sources from which legislation for the community of faith may be derived. Two sources were agreed upon: The Qur'ān and the sunna (practice of the Prophet). There was no disagreement in regard to the Qur'ān. However, opinions differed regarding what constituted the sunna. As the scholars around whom the schools were formed lived in different regions of the Islamic world, the differences among these schools were due largely to regional influences. But not only are these differences of little concern to Muslims, they are also seen as a sign of

mercy from God. The Prophet is reported to have said, "Difference of opinion in the community is a token of divine mercy."

There is no obligation to follow one school or another unless rulers or society choose to do so. In some cases—many countries of the Arab world—more than one school may be active. These schools are:

• The *Ḥanafi* School, founded by Abū Ḥanīfa—started in Iraq and became predominant in Persia (until its conversion to Shī'ism) and the East (Central Asia, India) and, following its adoption by the Ottoman Empire, wherever the Ottomans had authority;

• The *mālikī* School, founded by *al-imām* Mālik—started in Medina and became predominant in North and sub-Saharan Africa;

• The *Shāfi'ī* School, founded by *al-imām* al-Shāfi'ī—predominant in the Arab world;

• The *ḥanbalī* School, founded by *al-imām* Ibn Ḥanbal—now predominant, in its Wahhābī expression, in Saudi Arabia.

Differences in opinion among the schools arise from the degree of credence each school is inclined to give to such factors as the personal opinion of the judge, analogy, consensus, local custom or practice, the well-being of the community, and so forth, in the formulation of laws. The most influential scholar ("founder" of a school) in shaping the manner in which laws are to be derived was al-Shāfi'ī, whose school has been described as "moderate" and the "via media" between the "liberalism" of the Ḥanafīs and the "ultra-orthodoxy" of the Ḥanbalīs.

[10] The Ka'ba is the holiest sanctuary in Islam. It is believed to be a rebuilding of a temple built by Abraham for the worship of God. It is the point every Muslim faces (*qiblah*) at the time of prayer. Pilgrimage to Mecca and the circumambulation of the Ka'ba, at the appointed time, constitute the last of the five pillars of faith and the only noncompulsory one. The others are the *shahādah*, already mentioned, performing the five daily prayers (*alāt*), giving the ritual alms (*zakāt*), and fasting the month of Ramaḍān (*ṣawm*).

[11] The *sidr* was identified as "the species of lote-tree called . . . *rhamnus spina Christi* or *rhamnus nabeca*" (E. W. Lane, *Arabic-English Lexicon* [London, 1863; reissued 1984]). It is suggested by several scholars, Muslim and non-Muslim, that when steeped in water, the leaves of the lote-tree growing in cultivated land produce a perfume-like scent.

[12] Jesus holds a special position in the Qur'ān and, consequently, in Islam. He is a Prophet and a Messenger of God bearing the gospel. By God's command, he was born of the Virgin Mary but, contrary to the affirmation of the Christians, he was neither divine nor the Son of God. By God's command, Jesus healed the sick, raised the dead, and

breathed life into formed clay (birds). He taught righteousness and the worship of God and foretold the coming of Muḥammad. According to Islam, although people thought otherwise, Jesus was neither crucified nor did he die, but was ascended into heaven.

[13] While the descent of Jesus is not specifically mentioned in the Qur'ān, some interpreters have found evidence for him being a sign of the Hour in verse 43:57-64 and particularly verse 61. It is difficult to engage in an analysis of this evidence without reference to the Arabic text. The debate revolves around an Arabic pronominal suffix (third person, masculine, singular) in verse 61 and whether or not it should be understood as equivalent to "he," referring to Jesus, "He is a sign of the Hour," or "it," as the beginning of an affirmative sentence, "It is knowledge of the Hour."

[14] Several verses in the Qur'ān make reference to this eschatological event: 6:73, 18:99, 20:102, 23:101, 27:87, 36:51, 39:68, 50:20, 69:13 and 78:18. Of these, 69:13 specifies that it shall be a single blast, "So, when the Trumpet is blown with a single blast," while 39:68 alone suggests two blasts, "For the Trumpet shall be blown, and whosoever is in the heavens and whosoever is in the earth shall swoon, save whom God wills. Then it shall be blown again, and lo, they shall stand, beholding."

[15] Qur'ān, 17:71, 69:19, and especially 84:7-8.

[16] Qur'ān, 69:25 (in their left hand) or 84:10 (behind their back).

[17] The citation excludes the chorus cited above, which punctuates the passage in an inimitable, fast-moving, rhapsodic style.

[18] This is admirably discussed by Ernst Curtius in his work (in translation from the German) *European Literature and the Latin Middle Ages* (London: Routledge and Kegan Paul, 1953), pp. 195ff. The *locus amoenus* ("the place of pleasance") is a literary motif possessing its own "independent rhetorico-poetical existence." Curtius points out its existence in European literature from the Roman Empire to the sixteenth century. He describes it as "a beautiful, shaded natural site. Its minimum ingredients comprise a tree (or several trees), a meadow, and a spring or brook. Birdsong and flowers may be added" (p. 195). Curtius points out that "Virgil's description of the Elysian Fields was employed by Christian poets for Paradise" (p. 200).

4

Hinduism

Anantanand Rambachan

The Kaṭha Upaniṣad begins with the story of Vājaśravā, who is performing the Viśvajit ritual in which he is supposed to give away all his possessions. His young son Naciketā observes that his father is violating the requirements of the ritual by giving as gifts only those cows that are old and incapable of producing young. To draw his father's attention to his miserliness, Naciketā asks, "Father, to whom will you offer me?" His father does not respond, and Naciketā repeats his question three times. Finally, in an outburst of anger, Vājaśravā replies, "To Death I offer you."[1]

Naciketā reaches the abode of Yama, the lord of death, but finds that Yama is not there. With tremendous discipline and patience, he waits for three days and nights without food. Yama is very apologetic when he returns, concerned about the negative consequences of failing to welcome an honored guest with traditional hospitality. To compensate for this lapse, he offers Naciketā any three boons. For his first boon, Naciketā requests that his father be free from anxiety and from anger towards him. For his second boon, he asks for the details of a fire ritual for the attainment of the heavenly world. Yama readily grants these two boons.

The young boy's third request, however, fills Yama with surprise. "When a man dies," says Naciketā, "there is this doubt:

some say, 'It exists'; some again, 'It does not exist.' This I should like to know, being taught by you. This is the third of my boons." Since Naciketā has already asked for information about a ritual that leads to the heavenly world, he does not doubt the survival of some aspect of the human person after the death of the physical body. He is asking, therefore, for more precise knowledge of the entity that endures beyond death. Yama begs to be relieved of the burden of teaching about this subject because of its subtlety and difficulty of comprehension. "Ask for sons and grandsons," says Death, "who will live a hundred years, herds of cattle, elephants, horses and gold; choose a vast territory on earth, and live yourself as many years as you desire. . . . Here are these women with chariots and musical instruments—such indeed are not obtainable by mortals. With these, who are offered by me, you get yourself served. But do not ask anything again about death, O Naciketā."

Yama does eventually instruct Naciketā about the secrets of death, and many of his teachings I will share with you. I chose, however, to begin with the story of the meeting between Naciketā and Death for another reason. By using Death himself as the teacher in this text, the Upaniṣad intriguingly draws our attention to the fact that death may hold some of the most important secrets about life and that the human search for meaning is incomplete without an encounter with death. "Where can I find," asks Naciketā, "a better teacher than you?" The significance of life cannot be contemplated if one is unmindful of death.

There are other lessons from this story of Naciketā and Yama. Death does not reveal its secrets to one who does not seek with patience and persistence. Naciketā waits for three days at Yama's door without food. Even more important, Death does not reveal its secrets to the unreflective mind, which is still full of greed for the transient goods of the world. He teaches Naciketā only after Naciketā firmly rejects his offer of cattle, elephants, horses, gold, kingdoms, and long life, and explains his dissatisfaction with these. Death gives its secrets only to those who have ceased to cling to those things that death must eventually snatch away.

With Death as a teacher, one may expect that the student comes away with a depressing sense of life's finitude. In the case of Naciketā, however, Death teaches the way to eternal peace (*śāśvatī śāntiḥ*) and unending happiness. Instructed by Death, Naciketā became free from death (*vimṛtyuḥ*) in this life itself.

I will now selectively identify a few of the central features of the Hindu tradition for those unfamiliar with Hinduism and also in order to put into context the things I wish to say about life after death.

CENTRAL FEATURES OF HINDUISM

Hinduism is an astoundingly diverse tradition and this fact is suggested by name *Hindu* itself. Hindu is not the personal name of a founder or sage whose teachings are followed by members of this religion. It does not describe or identify a central doctrine or practice. "Hindu" is the Iranian variation for the name of a river that Indo-Europeans referred to as the Sindhu, Greeks as the Indos, and the British as the Indus. Those who lived on the land drained by the Indus river system were derivatively called Hindus. They did not necessarily share a uniform religious culture and the Hindu tradition continues to shelter a multiplicity of beliefs and practices. It reflects also the astonishing variation in geography, language, and culture across the Indian subcontinent. It is helpful to think of Hinduism as an ancient, large, and many-branched family, recognizable through vital common features, but preserving also the rich uniqueness of its individual members. If we are attentive to this fact of diversity and difference, then the generalizations I must make will not be misleading.

Many of the vital common features of the Hindu family can be traced to a body of knowledge known as the Vedas. The four Vedas (*Ṛg, Sāma, Yajur, Atharva*) are revered by orthodox Hindus as revelation and enjoy special authoritative status. Many other texts are regarded as revelation by particular Hindu groups, but the Vedas enjoy an almost unanimous recognition as a source of revealed knowledge. Each Veda may be broadly divided into two sections. The first section of each text is referred to as the *karmakāṇḍa* and provides information and rules for the performance of religious rituals. The last section of each text is referred to as the *jñānakāṇḍa* or the wisdom section. It contains a series of dialogues known as the Upaniṣads, which are the most important sources of religious and philosophical thinking in Hinduism. Any school of thought within Hinduism that values the stamp of orthodoxy tries to establish, through commentaries, that its interpretations are faithful to these dialogues. Therefore a tremendous body of secondary literature has developed around these texts. Most of the ideas I will share about life after death in Hinduism may be traced to these texts.

Contrary to many popular impressions, the Hindu tradition is neither life-denying or other-worldly. While it does not uphold the fulfillment of our material needs or the enjoyment of these gains as life's highest end, it has acknowledged their necessity and significance in the scheme of human life. Wealth (*artha*) and pleasure (*kama*) are among the four legitimate goals of human existence. While not rejecting the goals of worldly wealth and pleasure, the Hindu tradition repeatedly reminds its followers of the transient and uncertain quality of these two ends and of their inability to grant us lasting satisfaction. The first two goals of wealth and pleasure must also be sought by being responsive to the demands of the third goal, referred to as *dharma*. While *dharma* is a multifaceted concept and difficult to translate into a single English equivalent, it derives its meaning from the fact that every human being is inseparably connected with and dependent on other human beings as well as nonhuman realities. Like cells in a human body, we contribute to the whole while being nourished and sustained by it. The goal of *dharma* requires that we be attentive to the welfare of the whole even as we seek to meet our individual needs. We violate *dharma* when we obsessively and narrowly pursue private desires that destroy the harmony of the communities on which our lives depend.

While the Hindu tradition ascribes tremendous value to the goal of *dharma* and has discussed its requirements in minute detail, the tradition also sees this goal as having a transient quality. The focus of *dharma*, the community, is limited to a moment in time. As Huston Smith observes, "When time turns community into history, history, standing alone, is finite and hence ultimately tragic. It is tragic not only because it must end—eventually history, too, will die—but in its refusal to be perfected. Hope and history are always light-years apart."[2]

A human being who appreciates the necessity but also the transiency of wealth, pleasure, and duty, and who asks with intense sincerity whether there is anything of lasting value in existence, is ready to embark on the journey to Hinduism's ultimate and most valued goal, *mokṣa*. The Sanskrit term *mokṣa* means freedom, and if we recall the diversity of perspectives I mentioned earlier, it is not inaccurate to generalize here and to say that this freedom, in a primary sense, is from ignorance (*avidyā*). It is a common view of the Hindu tradition that ignorance of the true nature of the human self (*ātman*), God (*brahman*) and the world (*jagata*) is the fundamental cause of suffering and bondage. Freedom or liberation cannot be attained without right knowledge of reality.

For three of the great philosophers and traditions Hinduism, Śaṅkara (Non-dualism—Advaita), Rāmānuja (Qualified Non-Dualism—Viśiṣṭādvaita) and Madhva (Dualism—Dvaita), the self (*ātman*) cannot be equated or identified with the time-bound physical body or with the continuously changing characteristics of the mind. The self, in its essential nature, is eternal, uncreated, and free from all change. Consciousness and bliss constitute its essence. For Śaṅkara, the self is ultimately identical with *brahman*, for Rāmānuja it is inseparably related to *brahman* as body to soul or as part to whole, while, for Madhva, it is entirely different from but completely dependent on God.

Ignorant of its true nature, the self wrongly identifies its nature with the physical body and the mind, assumes the limitations of these, and becomes wanting and desireful. To attain the finite objects of its desires, it puts forth actions (*karma*) of various kinds. Desire-prompted actions generate results for which the performer of actions is responsible and which lead to subsequent rebirths in order to experience the consequences of these actions. All the traditions of Hinduism adhere firmly to a belief in the doctrine of *karma* as a law of cause and effect that includes the moral and spiritual dimensions of human life. While the doctrine of *karma* is often thought of in fatalistic terms, even by Hindus themselves, it emphasizes the fact and significance of human responsibility and choice. We tend, in the view of Hinduism, to focus too much on the unpleasant circumstances of our lives without considering how our own freely made choices might have brought us there and how new choices can liberate us. The belief in a cycle of multiple births and deaths, referred to as *saṁsāra*, is intrinsically related to the doctrine of *karma*. The latter affirms that every volitional action produces a result that is determined by the nature of the action and the motive which underlies it. Since births have been multiple, we can conceive of a storehouse of the effects of previous actions that cannot be exhausted in any single lifetime. Future births are thus necessitated for the purpose of experiencing the desirable and undesirable consequences of past and present lives and for the attainment of unfulfilled desires. In these future lives, of course, the effects of new actions are added to the storehouse of *karma* and the cycle of *saṁsāra* is perpetuated.

Mokṣa, in Hinduism, is consequent upon the right understanding of the nature of self. While, as we have seen, the self is understood differently within the tradition, *mokṣa* in all cases implies the recognition of the self to be different from the psycho-physical apparatus, to be free from the limitations of time, and to be blissful. Such an understanding of the self's essential nature brings an end to the cycle of birth, death, and rebirth. One who attains knowledge of the self is not reborn. For Śaṅkara, liberation is possible while the individual is alive in the body. When one knows the self, one ceases to identify with the body and is free. For Rāmānuja, on the other hand, the self can never recover its innate purity as long as it remains associated with the body. Freedom, therefore, in its true sense, must await the death of the body. For both philosophers, however, *mokṣa* also implies freedom from suffering, desire or want, and mortality.

HINDU VIEWS OF THE PERSON

It is useful to begin this discussion of Hindu views of life after death with an account of the way in which the tradition has described the constitution of the human being. I have introduced

encer, in the state of deep sleep, is aware only of ignorance (*ajñāna*).

It is important to reiterate that the self is different from all three bodies. In relation to them the *ātman* is knower and subject. It is unchanging awareness, while all three bodies are subject to fluctuation and change.

HINDU VIEWS OF DEATH AND AFTERLIFE

In the Hindu outlook, death may be properly thought of as the separation of the subtle body from the physical body. In the case of an unliberated individual, the subtle body, illumined by the consciousness that is the self, and consistent with its own *karma* and individual tendencies, will identify with another appropriate physical body. The Bhagavadgītā (2:22) in one of its well-known analogies compares death to the changing of clothing: "As, after casting away worn out garments, a man later takes new ones, so, after casting away worn out bodies, the embodied Self encounters other, new ones."[8]

This analogy is rich with suggestions, but I will draw your attention to only two of these. First, a suit of clothing is not identical with the wearer. Similarly, the changing physical body, which is likened here to clothing, is not the repository of the true identity of the human person. Second, there is the similarity of a continuity of being. When a suit of clothing is changed, the wearer continues to be, and with the death of the physical body, the indweller does not die. The subtle body is the link of continuity between the old and new bodies.

The Bṛhadāraṇyaka Upaniṣad (IV.iii.36) likens death in old age to the separation of a ripe fruit from its stalk and emphasizes that it not to be seen as an abnormal feature of human existence.

> When this [body] becomes thin—is emaciated through old age or disease—then, as a mango, or a fig, or a fruit of the peepul tree is detached from its stalk, so does this infinite being, completely detaching himself from the parts of the

> body, again go, in the same way that he came, to particular bodies, for the unfoldment of his vital force.[9]

The Bṛhadāraṇyaka Upaniṣad then goes on to describe the process by which the subtle body disengages itself from the physical body. The text offers a sequence, and it would be interesting if this sequence could be corroborated with studies and observation of the dying process.

> (The eye) becomes united (with the subtle body); then people say, "He does not see." (The nose) becomes united; then they say, "He does not smell." (The tongue) becomes united; then they say, "He does not taste." (The vocal organ) becomes united; then they say, "He does not speak." (The ear) becomes united; then they say, "He does not hear." (The Manas) becomes united; then they say, "He does not think." (The skin) becomes united; then they say, "He does not touch." (The intellect) becomes united; then they say, "He does not know."[10]

The Upaniṣads suggest that the actual point of exit of the subtle body from the physical body varies from person to person and is dependent upon the quality of the individual's spiritual consciousness at the time of dying. Kaṭha Upaniṣad II.iii.16 speaks of the nerves of the heart as being one hundred and one in number. One of these passes through the head. The exit of the subtle body through this nerve leads to the attainment of immortality. Exit through other parts of the body implies rebirth.[11]

One interesting suggestion of the Upaniṣads is that the new body to be assumed by the individual is already conceived in thought form as the subtle body disengages from the physical one. The analogy of Bṛhadāraṇyaka Upaniṣad IV.iv.3 provides a basis for such a view:

> Just as a leech supported on a straw goes to the end of it, takes hold of another support and contracts itself, so does the self throw this body aside—make it senseless—take hold of another support, and contract itself.

Śaṅkara, in this commentary on Brahmasūtra III.I.i, affirms that "the soul when passing from one body to another is enveloped by the subtle parts of the elements which are the seeds of the new body."[12] The elements that make up this potential body are referred to by Śaṅkara as the *bhūta sūkṣmas* or the subtle parts of the five gross elements and must be distinguished from the subtle elements as we have already described them. Rāmānuja, in his commentary on Brahmasūtra III.I.i also supports such a view.[13]

From the standpoint of Hinduism, there is every reason to assume that the subtle body is imbued with consciousness after its detachment from the physical body. Bṛhadāraṇyaka Upaniṣad IV.iv.2 describes it as having consciousness (*savijñāno bhavati*). We have seen earlier that it is made up of the five elements in an uncompounded form, and its seventeen parts include the five vital forces, the five senses, the five organs of action, the mind, and the intellect.

The pioneering research of Dr. Raymond Moody into the phenomena of near-death experiences indicates that the majority of his subjects describe themselves as being in another body after release from the physical one. If we keep in mind the complexities of this type of research and the problems of language in describing such experiences, the descriptions provided by Moody's subjects correspond in interesting ways with the characteristics attributed to the subtle body in Hinduism. The imperceptibility of the "spiritual body," as Moody calls the new body, may be explicable by the fact that it is composed of matter in a subtle form and thus inaccessible to the organs of the physical body. This may also explain its seeming lack of solidity and weightlessness. The ability to see, hear, and think in the new body is consistent with the presence of the subtle sense organs and the mind/intellect equipment. Subjects also report the experience of organs of action like the hands and legs. Severe damage to the physical body does not appear to cause adverse effects on the subtle one. Moody's subjects describe the ability to "pick up the thoughts" of persons around them. This may suggest a direct form of communication between one subtle body and another without the intervention of audible speech.[14]

The Upaniṣads, as indicated above, suggest that the point of exit of the subtle body from the physical body at the time of death is determined by the nature of the individual's consciousness. The texts also suggest that the journey and destiny of the individual after the death of the physical body are also determined by the same factor. The Hindu idea is that just as a person's thoughts, desires, hopes, and actions determine the course of his or her life before death, so do these factors also guide the individual's journey after death. This logical continuity between one life and another, as we have seen, is made possible by the persistence of the subtle body, the location of all unique individual personal traits.

The Bhagavadgītā (8:6) clearly teaches that the nature of one's existence after death is determined by the quality of one's consciousness at the time of death.

> Moreover, whatever state of being he remembers when he gives up the body at the end, he goes respectively to that state of being, Arjuna, transformed into that state of being.

Kṛṣṇa, the incarnate Lord, assures Arjuna that remembrance of him at the time of death leads to the attainment of his state of being. Arjuna must have no doubt of this.[15] There are numerous stories in the Hindu tradition that tell of the saving power of God's name at the time of death, and Hindus often recite such names near the dying person to focus his or her attention on God in the last moments. A popular story from the Bhāgavata Purāṇa tells the story of Ajamila, the brahmin who married a lowly servant girl. Ajamila became a social outcaste and earned his living by playing dice and stealing. He lived for eighty years and fathered ten sons, the youngest of whom was called Nārāyaṇa (a popular name for Viṣṇu). Ajamila loved Nārāyaṇa deeply and lavished wealth and attention on him. When the messengers of death approached him on his deathbed, Ajamila was overcome with fear and called out for his favorite son, Nārāyaṇa. By calling out the name of Nārāyaṇa, although his intention was to call his son and not God, Ajamila was saved from the messengers of death and taken to the realm of Viṣṇu.

While the intent of such stories is to emphasize correctly the extraordinary compassion of God, Hindu texts and teachers remind us that it is unlikely for one to think of God at the time of death if one has not been thinking of God throughout one's life. After teaching Arjuna in the Bhagavadgītā (8:6) that one attains a state of being consistent with one's mental condition at the time of death, Kṛṣṇa immediately implores him to strive to think of him at all times. This is the assured way to attain him after death. Commenting on Bṛhadāraṇyaka Upaniṣad IV.iv.2, Śaṅkara contends that the particular consciousness of the individual at the time of death is a consequence of past work and does not develop independently. One goes to the body that is related to that consciousness. Śaṅkara writes:

> Therefore, in order to have freedom of action at the time of death, those aspirants after the future life who have faith should be alert to the practice of the system of Yoga and right knowledge, and in the acquisition of particular merit (by doing good deeds). All the sacred books also carefully dissuade men from doing evil; for nothing can be done at the dying moment, since there is no independence for the man, who is carried away by his past work.[16]

In terms of the actual modes of being attainable after death, the Bhagavadgītā (9:25) makes mention of a number of these. Worshipers of the *devas* or presiding deities of various natural phenomena attain the *devas*. Those who are devoted to the *pitṛs* (departed ancestors) go to the ancestors. Devotees of the *bhūtas* (various good or evil spirits) reach these beings, while those who worship God attain God. From all of the first three worlds or states of being, one is eventually subject to rebirth. One returns even from the world of the lord of the *devas* (*svargalokaṁ*). This latter world is attained by those who desire it, have cleansed themselves of evil, and perform the appropriate religious rituals. While describing the vastness of this world and its celestial pleasures, the inevitability of return to the world of mortality, after the exhaustion of merits, is underlined.[17] The yearning for heavenly enjoyments and power, however magnified such gains may be, does not lead to freedom from the rounds of birth, death, and rebirth. Such desires and worlds still belong to the finite realm of cause and effect and are, therefore, finite.[18] Only the attainment of God assures freedom from return to the worlds of mortality.[19]

The Upaniṣads mention a number of possibilities, and many of these coincide with the options mentioned in the Bhagavadgītā. The world of heaven (*svargaloka*) and its limitations are acknowledged in the Upaniṣads. It is attained by those who desire it, believe in the existence of a body other than the physical one, and engage in good works of public charity and service. Kṛṣṇa also mentions *svargaloka* as the reward of the faithful performance of worldly duties.[20] The path to heaven, however, is still characterized as a path of darkness, because it does not presuppose knowledge of the true self and is subject to rebirth.[21] It is referred to in the Upaniṣads as the *pitṛyāna* or path of the ancestors.

The heavenly world, in the Upaniṣads, is conceived as a sphere of enjoyment earned by those who desire it through the performance of righteous actions. An individual does not accumulate new *karma* in this world. Upon the exhaustion of the effects of the meritorious actions, however, the individual enters again the cycle of birth, death, and rebirth. Chāndogya Upaniṣad (V.x.5,6) offers a description of the return or the rebirth of the individual.

> Having dwelt there till exhaustion, they return again, by the same path as they came, to *ākāśa*; from ākāśa to air; having become air, they become smoke; and having become smoke, they become mist.
>
> Having become mist, he becomes the cloud; having become the cloud, he becomes rain;—then he is born as rice, barley, herbs and trees, sesamum and beans. Henceforth, exit becomes extremely difficult, whoever eats food, and who sows the seed, he becomes like unto him.

In his commentary on Brahmasūtra (III.I.24), Śaṅkara contends that the references here to the individual's contact with various elements mean mere contact with these and not transformation into these forms. The body with which the returning individual is associated is determined largely by its store of unexhausted *karma*.

The Bhagavadgītā (6:37-44) offers a good example of the manner in which prior actions and mental states determine an appropriate rebirth from the heavenly world. Kṛṣṇa's answer is prompted by a question from Arjuna about the fate of an individual who fails to attain perfection in Yoga in spite of possessing faith. "Is he not," asks Arjuna, "lost like a disappearing cloud, having fallen from both worlds, having no solid ground, O Kṛṣṇa, confused on the path of Brahman?" Kṛṣṇa's response underlines the causal connection between the new physical body and past conduct.

> Attaining the worlds of the meritorious, having dwelt there for endless years, he who has fallen from yoga is born again in the dwelling of the radiant and illustrious.
>
> Or he may be born in the family of wise yogins; such a birth as this is very difficult to attain in the world.
>
> There he regains the knowledge derived from a former body, and he strives onward once more toward perfection, Arjuna.

The attainment of *svargaloka* by those who desire it and who are meritorious does not, it appears to me, preclude the possibility of rebirth immediately or within a short time after physical death.

While the Upaniṣads seem generally to propose that individuals returning from the heavenly world are reborn as human beings, there are indeed several texts which suggest rebirth after death in nonhuman physical forms. Chāndogya Upaniṣad (V.x.7), for example, mentions the possibility of rebirth as an animal, while Kaṭha Upaniṣad (II.ii.5) refers to rebirth in stationary forms. The function of such texts may be to inspire virtuous action, but they have also been interpreted as indicative of the real possibility of rebirth into these forms. It should be remembered, however, that in none of these forms is the individual capable of acquiring new *karma*. When the effects of unmeritorious actions have been exhausted, the individual returns to human life to continue the journey to *mokṣa*.

Another possibility mentioned in the Upaniṣads is the attainment of *brahmaloka* or the world of the creator. From *brahmaloka* there is no return to the world of rebirth. According to the Advaita (Non-dual) tradition, *brahmaloka* is attained by those who have sought God with intensity, but whose understanding of God is still conditioned and limited by human conceptions. They are worshipers of *brahman* thought of a possessing form and definable characteristics (*saguṇa brahman*). Such individuals abide in the world of *brahmaloka*, where they continue their spiritual journeys and come to understand God as the sole reality that transcends all human definitions and characteristics and ultimately non-different from the fundamental human self (*ātman*). At the time of cosmic dissolution, such individuals attain liberation. The path to *brahmaloka*, referred to in the Upaniṣads as the *devayāna* or way of the gods, is described in the Upaniṣads as a luminous path since one does not return to the world of mortality and attain liberation at the end of the creation cycle. It is a path of gradual liberation (*krama-mukti*); it involves a journey to *brahmaloka* and existence there until cosmic dissolution. This gradual way, as we will see, can be distinguished from *sādya-mukti* or immediate liberation in this life.

The Chāndogya Upaniṣad (IV.xv.5) specifically mentions that the attainment of *brahmaloka* does not depend upon the performance of funeral rites for the departed. The individual is escorted to the world of the creator by one who resides there.[22] It must be emphasized that the world of *brahmaloka* is available only to those who seek the eternal with faith, self-control and austerity. The Muṇḍaka Upaniṣad (I.ii.11) describes those who are qualified for this path.

> Those who live in the forest, while begging for alms—viz those (forest-dwellers and hermits) who resort to the duties of their respective stages of life as well as to meditation,—and the learned (householders) who have their senses under control—(they) after becoming freed from virtue and

> vice, go by the path of the sun to where lives that Puruṣa, immortal and undecaying by nature.

Even as there are pleasurable worlds that may be attained for temporary periods after the death of the physical body, there are also unpleasant worlds which may be similarly achieved. The Bhagavadgītā, for example, refers on four occasions to the disagreeable world of *naraka*. In the first chapter Arjuna expresses the fear that the loss of family traditions will lead to this world (I:42, 44) and in the sixteenth chapter, Kṛṣṇa speaks of *naraka* as the destiny of human beings possessing demonic qualities (16:16, 21). If the heavenly worlds are temporary because the meritorious actions that lead to their gain are finite, one must also assume that the unpleasant worlds are also transient because even evil actions have a finite character.

In the vision of the Upaniṣads, the highest destiny of the individual after death involves no journey or travel. For the individual who has come to understand the identity of the self (*ātman*) with the ultimate reality of all things (*brahman*), there is no departure. At the time of death the physical body disintegrates into its constituent elements and the subtle body, free from all egocentric characteristics that perpetuate its individuality, merges into the subtle elements. The self, transcending all dualities of space and time, abides as itself. Liberated in life with the body (*jivan mukti*), such a person is liberated in death without the body *(videha mukti*).

Many beautiful passages in the Upaniṣads describe this liberation in life. One of the most detailed is the description offered in Bṛhadāraṇyaka Upaniṣad IV.iv.6-7.

> Of him who is without desires, who is free from desires, the objects of whose desire have been attained, and to whom all objects of desire are but the Self—the organs do not depart. Being but Brahman, he is merged in Brahman.
>
> Regarding this there is this verse: "When all the desires that dwell in his heart are gone, then he, having been mortal, becomes immortal, and attains Brahman in this very

> body." Just as the lifeless slough of a snake is cast off and lies in the ant-hill, so does this body lie. Then the self becomes disembodied and immortal, becomes the Supreme Self, Brahman, the Light.

The Muṇḍaka Upaniṣad (II.ii.8, 9) employs a popular Hindu scriptural image:

> As rivers, flowing down, become indistinguishable on reaching the sea by giving up their names and forms, so also the illumined soul, having become freed from name and form, reaches the self-effulgent Being who is higher than the highest.
>
> Anyone who knows that supreme Brahman becomes Brahman indeed. In his line is not born anyone who does not know Brahman. He overcomes grief and rises above sin; becoming freed from the knots of the heart, he attains immortality.

Śaṅkara, in his commentary on Muṇḍaka Upaniṣad (III.ii.6), cites the Mahābhārata text, "Just as the footmarks of birds cannot be traced in the sky or of fish in the water, so is the departure of the illumined." Such a liberated person is not subject to rebirth.[23]

While the Upaniṣads offer descriptions, real or symbolic, of the *devayāna* and *pitṛyāna* paths, and even some descriptions of the corresponding worlds, they are hesitant to describe the liberated state. Human language, which is limited and dependent upon dualistic distinctions, is entirely inadequate to characterize the liberated state. In the words of Kaṭha Upaniṣad (I.iii.15), one is liberated from the jaws of death by knowing that which is "soundless, touchless, colorless, undiminishing and also tasteless, eternal, odorless, without beginning and without end." In the Bhadāranyaka Upaniṣad (II.iv.14) Yājñavalkya reflects on the futility of describing the non-dual state:

> When to the knower of Brahman everything has become the Self, then what should one smell and through what,

> what should one see and through what, what should one hear and through what, what should one speak and through what, what should one think and through what, what should one know and through what? Through what should one know That owing to which all this is known—through what, O Maitreyī, should one know the Knower?

If one point emerges clearly from the Hindu account of life after death, it is that life and death are points on a continuum. One does not attain an experience after the death of the physical body discontinuous with the quality of one's life in the physical body. At the time of death, the essential self (*ātman*), clothed with the subtle body, embarks on a journey, the destiny of which is determined by its acquired merits and demerits, its desires, tendencies, and capacities. Our life in this world cannot be ignored, since it is the stage that launches us into the next. With this general point in view, life after death, in the Hindu and particularly Upaniṣadic perspective, offers a number of possibilities.

If our lives have been brutish and our thoughts and deeds cruel and destructive, our journeys may take us to regions of darkness or rebirth in a subhuman form. Existence in these regions or states is not indefinite. When the effects of the actions that brought such a fall are exhausted, we return to human life to continue the onward journey. A second possibility is rebirth as a human being without a journey to any other region. This is conceivably the fate of a virtuous person who doubts the existence of other worlds or one whose store of merit and demerit is relatively balanced.

The third possibility, one we have considered in some detail, is the attainment of the heavenly world (*svargaloka*). This, as we have seen, is for those who are virtuous but who desire a pleasurable life in the hereafter as the reward of virtue. Life in *svargaloka* is immensely pleasurable but not eternal. When the fruits of meritorious deeds are exhausted, such individuals are reborn in the human sphere. *Svargaloka* is a realm of enjoyment and provides no opportunity for acquiring *karma* or for growth of any kind.

The fourth possibility is the journey to *brahmaloka*, the world of the creator from which there is no return to mortality. It is a luminous path for those who seek God for God's sake and provides the opportunity for loving communion with the personal God of one's choice. Since the experience of *brahmaloka* involves dualistic presuppositions, it is not considered ultimate by the Advaita or Non-dualistic tradition. In this realm, however, the individual has the opportunity for further spiritual growth, which culminates in the understanding of the identity between oneself and the self of God. This is the way of gradual liberation or *krama mukti*.

The fifth possibility involves no journey. It is the destiny of those who, in this life itself, come to know the identity of the *ātman* and *brahman*. Such rare persons are considered to be liberated even in the body. At the time of death, both the physical and subtle bodies are absorbed in their respective elements. The eternal, effulgent, and liberated self abides in its own nature.

Notes

[1] See Kaṭha Upaniṣad in *Eight Upaniṣads with the Commentary of Śaṇkarācārya*, 5th ed., trans. Swami Gambhirananda (Calcutta: Advaita Ashrama, 1965-66). *Iśa, Kena, Kaṭha*, and *Taittīriya* are in volume 1, and *Aitareya, Muṇḍaka, Māṇḍūkya and Kārikā*, and *Praśna* are in volume 2. Subsequent references to these texts are from the above source.

[2] Huston Smith, *The World's Religions* (San Francisco: Harper, 1991), p. 19.

[3] See, for example, *The Vedānta Paribhāṣa of Dharmarāja Adhvarīndra*, trans. Swami Madhavananda (Belur Math: Howrah: The Ramakrishna Mission Saradapitha, 1972), chap. 7.

[4] See also Kaṭha Upaniṣad II.2.1.

[5] *śrotrasya śrotraṁ manaso mano yad*
vāco ha vācaṁ sa u prāṅasya prāṅaḥ
cakṣuṣaś cakṣuḥ. . . .

[6] The five subtle elements are described in the Vedānta tradition as undergoing a complex process of division and combination, referred to as *pañcīkaraṇa*, to evolve into the five gross elements.

[7] The same vital force has been given five different names according to its different functions: *prāṇa, apāna, samāna, vyāna,* and *udāna.*

[8] *vāsāṁsi jirṅāni yathā vihāya*
navāni gṛhṇāti naro 'parāṇi
tathā śarīrāṇi vihāya jīrṇāny
anyāni saṁyāti navāni dehī

—See *Shrī Bhagavad Gītā,* trans. Winthrop Sargeant (Albany: State University of New York Press, 1993). Hereafter abbreviated *B.G.*

[9] See *The Bṛhadāraṇyaka Upaniṣad with the Commentary of Śaṅkarācārya,* trans. Swami Madhavananda (Calcutta: Advaita Ashrama, 1975). Hereafter abbreviated *B.U.*

[10] *B.U.* IV.iv.2.

[11] See also *Chāndogya Upaniṣad with the Commentary of Śaṅkara,* trans. Ganganatha Jha (Poona: Oriental Book Agency, 1942), VIII.vi.6.

[12] See *The Vedānta-Sūtras with the Commentary of Śaṅkarācārya,* trans. George Thibaut, 2 vols. (Delhi: Motilal Banarsidass, 1988), I, pp. 102-3. Hereafter abbreviated *V.S.*

[13] See *The Vedānta-Sūtras with the Commentary of Rāmānuja,* trans. George Thibaut (Delhi: Motilal Banarsidass, 1989).

[14] See Raymond A. Moody, Jr., *Life after Life* (New York: Bantam Books, 1977), chap. 2.

[15] *B.G.* 8:5.

[16] *B.U.* IV.iv.2, p. 491.

[17] *B.G.* 9:20-21.

[18] See *B.G.* 2:42-44.

[19] See *B.G.* 8:16.

[20] See *B.G.* 2:32, 37.

[21] See *B.G.* 8:26. Also Muṇḍaka Upaniṣad I.ii.10 and *V.S.* III.I.8.

[22] See *B.U.* VI.ii.15.

[23] Śaṅkara, in his commentary on Brahmasūtra III.3.32, admits the possibility of the rebirth of some liberated persons for the purpose of fulfilling particular missions entrusted to them by God.

5

Buddhism

Eva K. Neumaier-Dargyay

MANY LIVES—MANY DEATHS: THE BASIC ASSUMPTIONS

The Indian Context

The awareness of human mortality has affected Buddha Gautama, the historical Buddha whose life span is dated either from 566 to 486 B.C.E. or from 448 to 368 B.C.E., in a profound sense. At the outset of his spiritual journey he longed for that where there is no death. To overcome and transcend the agony of dying and the stages leading up to it—aging and sickness—took center stage in Buddhist soteriology. This longing for transcending death as ascribed by the oldest Buddhist texts to Buddha Gautama was embedded in a fabric of views regarding mortality and existence which were commonly held in the India of the sixth and fifth centuries B.C.E. These general beliefs rested on the assumption that life is an ever-changing but endless process, whereas death is only one of its recurring phases. The energy that kept this process going was seen in karma, literally "action." In Classical India this endless chain of lives was perceived as a curse rather than pleasant, as existence in itself was experienced as painful and unsatisfactory. Buddhism adopted the general Indian views of karma and of an endless cycle of lives and deaths and merged it with its own theoretical and philosophical ideas.

General Buddhist Views about the Nature of Existence

Unlike most other religions, Buddhism sees the authority of its texts resting in the fact that they render the experience of a human being, Buddha Gautama, and of all those beings who, like him, have achieved enlightenment. In one of the most ancient texts the Buddha is quoted as saying that his disciples should not believe his words because he had uttered them but only if the words withstand the scrutiny of reason and comply with their own experience. The style of Buddhist reasoning that reflects this position is exemplified in the following elaborations. The foundation of Buddhist thinking is given in the concepts of the fourfold noble truth and the twelve steps of interdependency. I shall characterize both briefly.

The texts report that on the night Buddha Gautama gained enlightenment he had an insight into the nature of human existence. This is condensed into the formula of the fourfold noble truth. In short, this formula says that existence as experienced by humans and other species is unsatisfactory and full of suffering. This suffering is caused by a desire for permanence and identity. Thus, if suffering is caused by desire, suffering will end when desire is dissolved; this is nirvana—deathless, inexplicable, beyond words and thoughts. To actualize nirvana, one ought to follow the so-called eightfold noble path divided into three aspects: ethics that respect all that exists in its own rights; insight into the nature of things; and cultivating the mind through meditation. The fourfold noble truth has become a kind of blueprint of Buddhist soteriology and has spawned a voluminous literature elaborating on these basic principles. These three modes of spiritual development resonate, as we shall see, throughout *The Tibetan Book of the Dead*, which is the most significant Buddhist text devoted exclusively to the theme of death.

The teaching of the fourfold noble truth is complemented with that of the interdependence of all phenomena of existence. In brief, it says that existence starts with a "desire-to-be," which is rooted in a misperception about the fluidity and ambiguity of all phenomena. The desire-to-be results in the unfolding of body, sense faculties, and mental capacities. Through the sense faculties contact with the outside world is established, resulting in sensations that make the individual "cling." Responding and clinging to the stimuli provokes activities, that is, karma, which causes further existences. Traditionally this process is divided into twelve steps. In general, Buddhism perceives the entire universe as a web of interdependent fleeting moments that constantly transform and reproduce themselves. There are no substances or essences (in the sense of scholastic philosophy) that provide islands of permanence in a sea of impermanence, a state of affairs that applies also to human beings. To the bewilderment of many non-Buddhists, Buddhism views the idea of a permanent mental essence embodied in the human (the "soul") as a tenet that cannot withstand logical scrutiny and that therefore must be rejected as unfounded. This is known as the Buddhist concept of "no-self."

Common Buddhist Views of Death and Dying

How can Buddhism reconcile the idea of rebirth, which amounts to a continuation of existence, with that of no-self? If there is no self, what is reborn? Buddhists were of course aware of the fact that there is a center that coordinates and reflects on the sensory data received by the individual and that there is such a thing as individuality that sets one individual apart from another. They never denied that. By observing and analyzing the human being (and also other living and sentient beings), they believed that they discovered an endless array of phenomena making up the individual. These can be divided into five basic categories: physical phenomena, emotions, sensory perceptions, responses to sensory perceptions, and consciousness. The "soul," as understood popularly, cannot be detected (they argued) among the phenomena making up these five categories. Nor can one argue that it could exist outside of these categories, or that it would be identical with any phenomena belonging to these five categories.

One has to think of these five categories as being like streams whose composition is constantly changing. The momentum in each stream drives the process forward and guarantees its continuation beyond the individual's death. In traditional Buddhist speech one may say neither that the reborn individual is the same as the one that passed away nor that it is independent or totally different from it. From the Buddhist point of view death is a more comprehensive transformation than one might bargain for. "I" am not reborn, but rather the result of what I have done in and with my life and lives. This moment of transformation provides an opportunity to move the process rapidly forward toward enlightenment. This is the point where *The Tibetan Book of the Dead* comes in. More than any other Buddhist text dealing with death, this one has become known in the West. I shall deal with it in detail later.

To contextualize the discussion of this text, a brief consideration of the Buddhist ideas of death and dying is necessary. The moment of death is characterized by a heightened awareness that not only surveys the now-ending life but that has also the ability to look beyond the restrictions of ordinary existence. The mind is alert at the moment of death and can therefore understand issues otherwise beyond its grasp. This heightened awareness offers the opportunity to embark on a spiritual "short cut" rather than the tedious slog through numerous lives otherwise and normally necessary.

The special acuity of the mind at the moment of death is expressed by terms that point to its luminosity. The myths of many cultures and civilizations equate the afterlife with an experience of light. Early as well as later Buddhist texts express such views by attributing a luminous quality to the mind in its nonconceptual and primordial state.[1] At the moment of death the dying becomes aware of it in the form of extreme luminosity. *The Tibetan Book of the Dead* introduces the various phases of after-death experience, among them the perception of luminosity, and instructs the person how to respond to them. But the position taken in *The Tibetan Book of the Dead* is not without opposition from within the Buddhist traditions.

DYING AND BEING REBORN IN THE VIEW OF THE TRADITIONS

Disagreement of the Traditions

All Buddhist traditions share some basic views regarding death, namely (1) at the moment of death physical components separate from mental components, which subsequently results in the body's decay; and (2) the stream of phenomena that makes up the four mental categories (emotions, sensory perceptions, responses to sensory perceptions, and consciousness) is driven by karma to seek an embodiment that suits its karmic makeup. Diversity and conflict of opinion arise with regard to questions such as the following: How do the mental components bridge the distance from the place of death to where the new embodiment is to happen? How can they "travel" without a bodily base? Does it take time for the mental components to reach the place of rebirth? If so, how much?

Pali Tradition

The Pali texts represent a fairly early stage in the development of Buddhist thinking. They endorse the commonly accepted views regarding death but assume that the mental components, because of their immaterial nature, are not bound by the constraints of space and time and that therefore they face no resistance in overcoming distance as characteristic of a material body. Consequently, the Pali tradition denies that any time elapses between the moment of death and the new embodiment. Death and rebirth, in the form of conception, follow each other without interruption.

Buddhaghosa, the great commentator and interpreter of the Pali tradition, illuminated the process of death and rebirth through several parables found in his encyclopedic work *Visuddhimagga*.[2] He says that the disintegration of the five categories of the previous life and their formation in the one coming to be can be compared to the reciting of a text by the teacher, which is repeated in the disciple's mouth. In another analogy, it is like the flame of a candle igniting another candle. In both cases an earlier process comes to an end, yet provokes another process that has structural similarity to the first one. Buddhaghosa insists that nothing of the previous life continues in the next one. He compares the instantaneousness of rebirth with the sensory process wherein recognition in visual consciousness follows sensory awareness without a time gap. Thus, the Pali tradition does not know about an intermediary state (Tibetan: *bar do*) that can be a locus for the drama that unfolds in *The Tibetan Book of the Dead.* It would be wrong, however, to assume that all the Nikaya traditions (often referred to as Hinayana schools) share this view.

Abhidharmakosha Tradition

Like the *Visuddhimagga*, the *Abhidharmakosha* is an encyclopedia of Buddhist knowledge and practice, and both date roughly from the fifth century C.E. Nevertheless, the first synthesizes the thoughts of the Pali tradition and the latter those of the late Sarvastivadin tradition with an influence from Sautrantika point of view (both being Nikaya traditions that preferred the Sanskrit idiom over Pali).[3] The *Abhidharmakosha* addresses all those topics that form the core of the teaching of *The Tibetan Book of the Dead.* In particular it details the concept of the intermediary state (Sanskrit: *antarabhava*; Tibetan: *bar do*) as the five categories (physical phenomena, emotions, sensory perceptions, responses to sensory perceptions, and consciousness) as one between two destinations—the past life and the one to come.[4] Furthermore, the *Abhidharmakosha* attributes several characteristics to the intermediary being: it is visible only to creatures of similar spiritual accomplishment; it has complete sensory faculties (whereby the tactile bodily feelings are of an illusionary nature); it is unencumbered by material obstacles and distances. However, unlike *The Tibetan Book of the Dead*, which assumes that the intermediary being has the ability to affect rebirth or avoid it all together, the *Abhidharmakosha* views the path of the intermediary being as predestined by its karma. Thus, while Buddhaghosa viewed death as the end of one process (although instigating another one, rebirth), the *Abhidharmakosha* assumes a continuation of the idiosyncratic structure of the five categories beyond death, although in a drastically transmuted nature. What is emphatically denied by Buddhaghosa (although it is vicariously acknowledged in the *Abhidharmakosha*) is that something is transmitted from the life which has come to an end to that which is about to begin.

Mahayana Perspective

This trend increased and resulted in some Mahayana texts, such as the *Bodhisattvabhumi*[5] or *Vijñaptimatratasiddhi*[6] and related texts affirming the concepts of an intermediary state and of a being that dwells in this state. This being is like a clone of the deceased one, so that it can relive some of the experiences of the former. The only theme discussed in these Mahayana texts is the modality of the transmutation of the five categories of the deceased into those of the intermediary being and into the reborn one. Doctrinally these views were authenticated by referring to canonical accounts of advanced disciples who actualized nirvana after death while dwelling in a state that resembled the intermediary state.

The Tibetan Tradition

The Tibetan tradition weaves all these elements into a fabric that renders a powerful vision of what life and death mean to a person in quest for nirvana. The teachings of *The Tibetan Book of the Dead* are unquestionably rooted in Mahayana thinking. Its metaphors may sometimes be drawn from ancient inspirations, but its philosophical and soteriological thinking is intrinsically Buddhist by nature.

THE TIBETAN LORE OF DYING AND REBIRTH

Based on the description of the funeral rites practiced at the time of the Imperial Dynasty of Tibet (historic period from 618 to 842 C.E.), Tibetan culture seems to have a fascination with death and mortality.[7] Listing some details of the funeral rites from that period will illustrate the point.

The bodies of the deceased members of the Imperial family were subjected to several stages of funeral rites that stretched over years. Soon after death the intestines were separated from the body and often mixed with gold dust to be stored in special containers, while the corpse either underwent mummification or was exposed so that the flesh would fall off the bones. Finally the various human remains were taken in an elaborate procession to a tomb that resembled in its splendor and treasures (although not in size) the Egyptian pyramids.[8] Unfortunately, the tombs were opened by grave robbers shortly after the demise of the Imperial Dynasty in the ninth century, and the cultural and political situation of modern Tibet has not permitted archeological excavations of the tombs, which are considered sacred sites, not to be touched. Unlike other Asian cultures, Tibetan culture provided a fertile ground for the Buddhist ideas of death and dying to grow into a coherent lore for the living to prepare themselves for the moment of death. They find their most prominent expression in the *Tibetan Book of the Dead* (Tibetan title: *Bar do thos grol, Liberation from the Intermediary State by Means of Hearing This Lore*).

Textual Basis

In contemporary discussions of Tibetan texts dealing with death and funeral rites different genres have been conflated under the umbrella term "book of the dead," resulting in assumptions that there are several different Tibetan books of the dead.[9] The few editions of the Tibetan text *Bar do thos grol*, commonly but inaccurately known as *The Tibetan Book of the Dead*,[10] indicate that there is a cycle of texts whose core is identical, while the number of secondary texts may vary. This text, which instructs the dying how to understand the visions and perceptions that will occur immediately after the moment of death, has to be distinguished from other Tibetan texts that are used in funeral rites. The *Bar do thos grol* is used only by some followers of the Old

School (*rNying ma pa*) and the *bKa' brgyud pa* School of Tibetan Buddhism and some individuals of other Schools.

Rituals Guiding the Dead into the Afterlife

In the world of Tibetan culture there seems to be a great diversity of funeral rites varying from regions and religious tradition. To illustrate this point I shall summarize field observations I made in Zanskar, a valley in southern Ladakh, in 1979.[11] I was attending the funeral of an elderly man who was affiliated with a *dGe lugs* monastery. In this case the corpse, which was tied in a fetal position and clothed in the deceased's garb, was adorned with the emblems of the five Buddhas who are often referred to in Western literature as the Adi Buddhas. Monks from the nearby *dGe lugs* monastery surrounded the body. With recitations from the *Guhyasamaja tantra* they addressed the dead as "Buddha." Once the body was placed on the pyre, the monks—with the exception of two tantric adepts—went back to the monastery, while the supervision of the cremation was handed over to a fellow clan member. My question whether the use of the *Bar do thos grol* had ever been considered was answered by saying that this village was associated with a *dGe lugs* monastery and thus would not use this text.

Present ethnographic knowledge of Tibet is too sketchy to permit any general statement on funeral rites and the texts used in them. This, however, should not be used to minimize the significance of the *Bar do thos grol* as one of the great literary works of humanity on the experience of death.

THE *BAR DO THOS GROL*

Transmission of the Text

The *Bar do thos grol* (*Liberation from the Intermediary State by Means of Hearing This Lore*) belongs to the genre of so-called *gter ma* or treasure texts.[12] It consists of works, tradition claims, composed or at least inspired by Padmasambhava. In the Tibetan literature of the fourteenth century this Indian tantric master became a symbolic figure credited with acculturizing Indian Buddhism to meet the idiosyncracies of eighth-century Tibet. The historicity of Padmasambhava has become an issue of scholarly debate inside and outside Tibet. Regardless of what position one takes on this issue, the treasure texts draw their authority from Padmasambhava and the religious significance invested in him by Tibetan traditions. Only the followers of the Old School (*rNying ma pa*) and of the *bKa' brgyud* School consider treasure texts as authentic religious texts (with some exceptions from the *dGe lugs pa*).

According to indigenous accounts, Tibetans of the eighth century, that is, during the time when Padmasambhava dwelled in Tibet, were not mature enough to understand them. So Padmasambhava hid them in the hollow core of temple statues, in the attics of temples and shrines, and, more commonly, in caverns and crags of the mountain faces. He left behind prophecies foretelling when they would be discovered and which master would find the hidden treasure. The finding of treasure texts and their subsequent interpretation (the original is often reported to be written in an obscure script) was believed to be inspired and guided by visions and symbolic dreams.

Most treasure texts were found from the early fourteenth century onward and their discovery resulted in a massive and still little studied literature. The *Bar do thos grol* is one of these texts. It forms the centerpiece of a larger literary cycle known as *The Spontaneous Liberation through Contemplating the Peaceful and Wrathful Deities* (*zhi khro dgongs pa rab gsal*).

The *Bar do thos grol* and Its Discoverer

The tantric master Karma-gling-pa (born between 1326 and 1386) is credited with discovering the text at mountain sGampo-gdar, whose exact location remains unknown.[13] The text is extant in manuscripts and xylographs; it became more widely accessible through an Indian reprint in 1969.[14] No critical edition has ever been attempted, and the history of the text's development remains unknown to us.

Nevertheless, in the West the *Bar do thos grol* is certainly the most widely known Tibetan text. It has been translated into various European languages, and some editions spawned secondary translations, many of them being reprinted continuously.[15] Much of the popularity of the text is attributed to C. G. Jung's psychological commentary on the text, which is usually incorporated in the reprints of Evans-Wentz's translation. Jung sees the *Bar do thos grol* as substantiating his own claim that Freudian psychoanalysis never goes beyond the level of sexual fantasies, though the extent to which Jung did justice to Buddhist ideas needs to be examined carefully. For instance, without any further attempt to qualify his decision he replaces the Buddhist term "mind" (Tibetan: *sems*) with "soul," thereby neglecting to give credence to the Buddhist stance that explicitly denies such a concept.[16]

The Teaching of the Text

The *Bar do thos grol* consists of three parts:

1. Realization of the primordial luminosity at the moment of death (the intermediary state of death, *'chi kha'i bar do*);
2. Realization of true being in the forms of peaceful and wrathful deities (intermediary state of true being, *chos nyid bar do*);
3. Preventing rebirth in this world (intermediary state of becoming, *srid pa'i bar do*).

These parts are preceded by an introduction explaining for whom the text was composed and when it should be recited. I shall now introduce each of these three parts in more detail.

One who gained enough spiritual insight and practice in life will become aware of the primordial luminosity at the moment of death and recognize it immediately as indistinguishable from his or her own mind in its purity and from emptiness. This refers to the unspeakable and unthinkable that, in contemporary intellectual discourse, is often called the "semiotic" and that forms the base for the overdetermination and ambiguity of existence. Such a person will not go into the intermediary state but actualize nirvana. The perception of luminosity, however, is not restricted to these people only. On the contrary, every dying person will experience it, but persons of lesser spiritual experience will realize it only for an instant and may be frightened by it. Usually the experience of luminosity lasts "for not longer than it takes to finish one's meal" after the "external breath" has ceased but while the "inner breath" is still there. The concept of an "inner breath" is quite common in Indian thinking. It denotes the life force that is thought to be breath-like and travels in three pathways parallel to the spine. It sustains but also influences mental activity. The "inner breath" is often compared to a steed on which the mind rides. The concepts of "inner breath" and "pathways" underlie much of the teaching of the *Bar do thos grol.* When death is about to occur, the life force retreats into the central pathway and escapes through the crown of the head. This procedure is known as ejecting the mind (*'pho ba*). Some persons practice ejecting the mind during lifetime so that at the moment of death the mind will leave the body with no hesitation or interference from fear. Tradition has it that the person who masters this meditation will be able to induce death at will.

If the one dying has not achieved this level of spiritual development, then the spiritual teacher (this may be a monk, a nun, or a qualified lay person) will continue to read the *Bar do thos grol*, telling the dying one how to interpret the visions that are about to appear. This phase is known as the "intermediary state of being-as-such" (*chos nyid bar do*). The first vision after that of the indistinguishable primordial light is a light of utmost brilliance manifesting as the five Buddhas (*rigs lnga*), each of whom has his own color, cardinal direction, and wisdom as a kind of attribute. Their colorful images are bathed in such brilliant light that it dazzles the eyes of the dead. Each Buddha's compassion acts like a rescue hook with which the dead is pulled from the intermediary state while the wisdom of the Buddha, symbolized in his consort, pushes from behind. Obviously, the Tibetans as a mountain people saw the journey through the intermediary state as similar to a demanding scramble across rock cliffs. Each Buddha of the pentade (*rigs lnga*) appears in peaceful form first and later in a wrathful aspect. Each time he is accompanied by appropriate entourages. If one is not acquainted with Buddhist iconography, the visual representation of the wrathful forms of the Buddhas can be mistaken for demons or devils. Nevertheless, despite their appearance, the wrathful deities embody the utmost compassion of the Buddha. The ferocious appearance is meant to arouse persons from their stupor so that they can progress on the path toward enlightenment.

The third part, the intermediary state of becoming, is clearly separated from the first two parts of the text through a colophon (a paragraph identifying the author and scribe of the text). In content, the third part is different insofar as it deals with memory fragments of past life and how the dead one's emotional response to these memories lays the foundation for the emergent life. The style is also quite different. The first two parts use the serene language of meditation texts, while the third part dramatizes the dead one's visions as realistic nightmares. We read of hounds hunting down the dead, blinding blizzards making them run for shelter, and of soldiers and bandits poised to mutilate and dismember them. One of the first issues this part addresses is the perception that there is a bodily awareness in the mind of the dead person. The dead person is portrayed as having a bodily awareness that, on the one hand, mirrors his or her previous body while, on the other hand, it foreshadows the next. This "apparition body" provides the dead with sensations of sorrow, fear, and desire, but unlike the physical body, it is not bound by the restrictions of time and space. It can cover distances quickly and penetrate physical obstacles as if they were nonexistent. It can observe the world of the living and respond to it emotionally, but it cannot make itself heard by the living, who are unaware of the dead person's presence. Thus, the dead person feels isolated, frustrated, and in despair, because he or she does not understand that former friends and relatives do not know his or her fate. The dead person is advised as follows:

> Don't cling to these apparitions whatever they may be; don't yearn or pine for them! If, however, you yearn full of desire for them, then, you shall fall into the midst of pain as

> you wander among the six forms of existence (i.e., gods, titans, humans, animals, hungry ghosts, denizens of hell). Although you had been exposed to the intermediary state of true being, you did not grasp its sense, and now you must wander around here. If you can now find the strength to surrender to suchness (i.e. things as they are), then, you will realize the nature of mind in its luminosity as void, naked, and consuming as your spiritual teacher had taught you before. Remain with calm composure in this state which is without sensory perception and activity. Thus, you will not enter a womb but realize liberation.[17]

If the dead cannot remain in this state of equilibrium, he/she is advised to concentrate on the spiritual teacher in the appearance of his/her tutelary deities floating above his/her corona. But if the karmic inheritance is too weighty, then the dead will be drawn deeper and deeper into reliving crucial events of the past life that shape his/her future embodiment. Sensations of desire, hatred, and ignorance begin to dominate. The text adjusts its advice to suit the decreasing mental and spiritual potential of the dead. If the dead cannot understand that emptiness in its luminosity is the true nature of being, and that the visions of the five Buddhas and of his/her teachers and tutelary deities are its manifestation, then rebirth is inevitable. The only means to assist the dead is to provide guidance for rebirth that furthers spiritual development and reduces exposure to pain.

The pitiful sensations of the dead are described vividly as follows:

> You will feel cornered, irritated and cheated; your intellect is distracted, scattered and diffuse. At this moment you will only think "I'm dead. Just what can I do?" and while you become aware of these thoughts you will immerse yourself in self-pity. In this way you will suffer immensely. Don't feel attached to any one place because you have to wander around. Keep this in mind! Don't try to do this and that but let your mind be in complete equilibrium. The time

> will come when you will have nothing to eat but offerings of the funeral rites and when you cannot any longer rely on your friends. These are the signs that you as an apparition body are about to wander through the intermediary state of becoming.

If the dead cannot heed this advice, then he/she has to face the weighing of his/her previous acts, which the text stages as a court hearing. Yama, the god of death, presides as judge over the court, and his hangmen drag the dead in with a noose around the neck. In a mirror the acts that the dead person committed during life are revealed. Since evil deeds outnumber good ones, the dead person is sentenced to being dismembered. Although sensing the pain of having limb by limb severed from the body, the dead one cannot die because he/she is already dead and the present body is only an apparition. Nevertheless, the dead one may turn the tide even at this late moment if he/she recognizes that the torturers' innate nature is nothing but emptiness and a projection of the dead one's own mind. Finally, images of people engaged in sexual activities arise. The dead feel aroused and attracted to the mother and repulsed by the father if the dead one is to be reborn as a man, and attracted to the father and repulsed by the mother if he/she is to be reborn as a woman.

This last element drew much attention, particularly from psychoanalysts, since it appears to support some of Freud's observations regarding the Oedipal complex. If the dead one finds the strength to distance himself or herself from these sensations and recognizes them as illusions, then the "gateway to the womb" may still be closed.

The last paragraph of the text states that one should read, memorize, and recite it during one's life so that one will never forget its message "even if one is chased by seven hounds." It assures the reader that, if the text is remembered at the moment of death, rebirth can be avoided even by those of marginal spiritual practice. Overall, the teaching of the *Bar do thos grol* is intended to instill confidence and trust, so that the moment of death may lose some of its frightening appearance.

THE "LIBERATION FROM THE INTERMEDIARY STATE" AND REPORTS OF NEAR-DEATH EXPERIENCES

The *Bar do thos grol* has received revived attention in recent years in some measure because reports about near-death and clinical death experiences have revealed striking similarities with some of the visions and perceptions described in the Tibetan text.[18] This chapter is not the place to deal with these reports in detail nor to discuss whether these perceptions are physical or metaphysical. Here it may suffice to say that underneath a cultural articulation of the phenomena that characterize the death experience seem to lie some primary and transcultural phenomena. The most significant ones are the perception of brilliant light, the sensation of seeing one's old body, observing relatives and friends in their responses to one's death, and the feeling of being not confined by the materiality of a physical body while continuing to have a kind of bodily sensation. How one responds to and interprets such phenomena appears to be a matter of culture, belief, and personal disposition. Thus, some may perceive the brilliant light as the comforting image of Buddha or Christ. Others may be frightened by it.

Notes

[1] *Anguttara Nikaya*, ed. A. K. Warder (London: Pali Text Society, 1961 vol. 1), 1.6; *The Lankavatara Sutra*, trans. D. T. Suzuki (1932; repr. London: Routledge & Kegan Paul, 1966), p. 68; E. Conze, *Prajnaparamita Literature* (The Hague: Mouton, 1963), pp. 9 ff.; and D. S. Ruegg, *La Theorie du Tathagatagarbha et du Gotra* (Paris: École Française d'Extrême-Orient, 1969), pp. 411ff.

[2] Buddhaghosa's contribution to the formation of the Pali tradition is discussed by K. R. Norman in *Pali Literature—Including the Canonical Literature in Prakrit and Sanskrit of all the Hinayana Schools of Buddhism, A History of Indian Literature*, ed. Jan Gonda, vol. 7,2 (Wiesbaden: Otto Harrassowitz, 1983), pp. 120ff. The quoted parables are found in Buddhaghosa's *Visuddhi-Magga oder der Weg zur Reinheit*, trans. Nyanatiloka (Konstanz: Verlag Christiani, 1952), p. 721.

[3] Details about the *Abhidharmakosha* and its alleged author, Vasubandhu, are presented by Hirakawa Akira in *A History of Indian Buddhism from Sakyamuni to Early Mahayana*, trans. Paul Groner, *Asian Studies at Hawaii* 36 (Hawaii: University of Hawaii Press, 1990), pp. 136-38.

[4] Louis de La Vallee Poussin, *L'Abhidharmakosa de Vasubandhu, traduction et annotations, Melanges Chinoises et Bouddhiques* 16 (Brussels: Institut Belge des Hautes Études Chinoises, 1971), vol. 2, p. 33.

[5] Nilanaksha Dutt, ed., *Bodhisattvabhumi* (Patna: K. P. Jayaswal Research Institute, 1966), p. 269.

[6] Louis de La Vallee Poussin, trans., *Vijñaptimatratasiddhi: La siddhi de Huan-tsang* (Paris: Librairie Orientaliste Paul Geuthner, 1928), vol. 1, pp. 191, 200, 358, 401.

[7] Several scholarly works cover the historical development of that time: Paul Pelliot, *Histoire ancienne du Tibet* (Paris: Adrien Maisonneuve, 1961); Jacques Bacot, *Introduction a l'histoire du Tibet* (Paris: Société Asiatique, 1962); David Snellgrove and Hugh Richardson, *A Cultural History of Tibet* (London: Weidenfeld and Nicolson, 1968). The most recent and up-to-date discussion of early Tibetan history is by Christopher I. Beckwith, *The Tibetan Empire in Central Asia: A History of the Struggle for Great Power among Tibetans, Turks, Arabs, and Chinese during the Early Middle Ages* (Princeton: Princeton University Press, 1987).

[8] The Tibetan text recording these funeral rites was edited and translated by Giuseppe Tucci, *The Tombs of the Tibetan Kings*, Serie Orientale Roma I (Rome: Istituto Italiano per il Medio ed Estremo Oriente, 1950). The myths reflecting on the death of the emperors are discussed by Erik Haarh, *The Yar-lun Dynasty. A Study with Particular Regard to the Contribution by the Myths and Legends to the History of Ancient Tibet and the Origin and Nature of Its Kings* (Copenhagen: G. E. C. Gad's Forlag, 1969).

[9] This opinion is expressed, for instance, by Detlef I. Lauf, *Geheimlehren Tibetischer Totenbücher* (Freiburg I. Br.: Aurum Verlag, 1975), p. 13.

[10] See Dieter Michael Back, *Eine Buddhistische Jenseitsreise: Das sogenannte "Totenbuch der Tibeter" aus philologischer Sicht* (Wiesbaden: Otto Harrassowitz, 1979), p. 12.

[11] With great gratitude I acknowledge here the financial and institutional support I received from the Deutsche Volkswagenstiftung (Ger-

man Volkswagen Foundation), which enabled me to carry out these studies.

[12] For a comprehensive discussion of this literary genre see E. M. Dargyay, *The Rise of Esoteric Buddhism in Tibet* (1977; repr. Delhi: Motilal Banarsidass, 1979), pp. 62-81.

[13] The brief biography of Karma-gling-pa reports that he found the *Bar do thos grol* when he was fifteen years of age. He entrusted the teaching and the text to his disciples and in part to his son. He imposed the restriction that the teachings ought not to be disclosed to more than one person for the next three generations. After that time the teaching became widely spread in the eastern part of Tibet, that is, Amdo (Dargyay, pp. 151-53).

[14] Details about the various manuscripts and xylographs are found in Back, pp. 12-17.

[15] The most popular but least accurate translation is by W. Y. Evans-Wentz, *The Tibetan Book of the Dead* (1927; repr. London: Oxford University Press, 1972). The Italian Tibetologist G. Tucci presented a scholarly translation into Italian that reflected the understanding of the time, *Il libro Tibetano dei morti* (*bardo thodol*) (Turin: Unione Tipografico-Editrice Torinese, 1972). A few years later I translated the text for the first time into German (Eva K. Dargyay, *Das tibetische Buch der Toten* [Bern: Otto Wilhelm Barth Verlag, 1977]). F. Fremantle and Chogyam Trungpa rendered a more contemporary English translation, *The Tibetan Book of the Dead* (Boulder: Shambhala, 1975). The most recent translation is by R. A. Thurman.

[16] C. G. Jung, "Psychological Commentary," in Evans-Wentz, pp. xxxviii-xxxix. Some of the problems surrounding Jung's understanding of "soul" in this context had been identified by James Kirsch, the translator of Jung's commentary into English (p. xxxv).

[17] This quote and the ones to follow are my own translation from the Tibetan text.

[18] The most influential works are by Raymond A. Moody and Elisabeth Kübler-Ross.

6

Chinese Religions

Gary Arbuckle

NOTES FROM THE NETHER WORLD

> Don't proclaim that with the advances of science, ghosts and spirits have been reduced to nonexistence! . . . Sages and Buddhas, ghosts and spirits are the main moving power within the dark world, man is the one who is being moved.[1]

Vancouver prides itself on being a multicultural city, but that does not mean that there are not still many things on the shelves of a Chinese supermarket whose significance is opaque to the visitor from outside: unlabeled packages with ambiguous contents, inviting boxes whose exact terms of invitation are hidden from anyone ignorant of the ideographic script. Beside the pickled this and salted that at my local store, there is another half-shelf of miscellaneous material that at first sight seems more familiar. Pride of place there goes to package upon package of mock money: gold coins and ingots made of gilded paper, and colorful banknotes in improbably large denominations. "Monopoly money, party treats?" was the tentative identification of one non-Chinese woman I saw standing before that shelf a few weeks ago. Then she read the package, put it back, and walked away without looking back.

Something to bring an international touch to Park Place and Baltic Avenue? Not quite, as the woman's reaction might indicate. No doubt she had belatedly observed that these bills were drawn on no ordinary account, but rather on the Bank of Hell, as proclaimed in both English and Chinese across their tops. Below, instead of Her Majesty or some dead worthy from Canadian history, there was the portrait and signature of the king of hell himself, Yanluo Wang, the best known of the ten kings who judge and punish the deceased in the prisons of the Murky Country—to give a more accurate translation for *mingguo*, rendered "Hell" above. Beside that infernal money on the shelf there were passes and passports to present to the officials of the next world, funeral candles and incense, paper clothes to be burned lest the indigent among the dead suffer from cold—even credit cards, checks, and bankbooks to keep track of one's balance when trafficking with the residents of the next world. In short, the demands of the dead form an almost exact parallel to those of the living, or rather to those the living would have had in a milder, more humanized form of the China of late Imperial times: goods to supply daily needs, documents to deflect official wrath, and plenty of cash on hand for the dead to use as presents and bribes to ease purgatorial pains, and for the living to buy quittance from ghostly but nevertheless importunate strangers.[2]

Despite differences in detail introduced by historical change and the evolution of religious and philosophical ideas over three millennia, the sameness of the "other world" dominates Chinese conceptions of the afterlife. It has undoubted charms: familiarity, and the sense one could always work something out. But it also possesses a stifling grip that both ancients and moderns have on occasion attempted to evade: the powers that be are the powers that will be, forever and ever, world without end.

COSMOLOGICAL CONTEXTS AND THE THEORY OF THE SOUL

> Jilu asked about the service of ghosts and spirits. Confucius replied, "You have never been able to serve people. On

what basis would you serve ghosts?" "I venture to ask about death." "You have never understood life. On what basis would you understand death?"[3]

As the words of the Master indicate, death in ancient China was seen as no more than one part of a seamless whole, a universal order that should be approached and apprehended in proper sequence. A few words about that order are necessary to contextualize its infernal subdivision and elucidate some of the assumptions that shaped thought about both the dead and the living.

One favorite label for ancient Chinese thought is "this-worldly." This is strictly true, but unfortunate in its implications, for the most fundamental truth about the premodern world view is that there *is* no other world, properly speaking, no supernatural. The cosmic order is unitary, organic. It has no outside, it was never created, and it will never be destroyed; its "laws" are regularities dictated by its nature, not inviolable commands laid on it by some absolute divine Other. Being one and interconnected, its paramount need becomes harmony: discord automatically brings retribution, though the power of the various divine and infernal beings inhabiting it can ward off these consequences to a certain extent, and a human with enough knowledge of its workings can manipulate its balances in his or her favor.

Since at least the time of Confucius (fifth century B.C.E.) it has been widely accepted that, in a cosmic system which is intrinsically in balance, all irregularities and evils must come from the wrong exercise of human free will, since the human being is the only part of the cosmos endowed with freedom of choice. Thus, the responsibility for the maintenance and restoration of harmony lies in the human realm in the broadest sense, including divinities and spirits originally human.[4] By definition, this is where the problem must be located.

Life itself is a virtually unquestioned good, at least until the arrival of Buddhism; and the perception that Buddhism held a negative attitude toward life would become one of its most controversial points in China.[5] All indigenous schools of thought valued life and concentrated on its preservation; there was a low opinion of martyrdom, unless death was absolutely necessary to preserve the greater health of society.[6] To have to die for morality was often seen more as an unavoidable misfortune than a sought-for and glorious end.[7] The good person died in his or her bed; that is, in the family context that supplied the model both for the ideal polity and the world to come.

Around the end of the fourth century B.C.E., we have the first clear statement of what was to become the standard theory of the soul. According to this, conception created a soul called the *po*, a word that may be related to others with the general meaning of "control" or "oversee."[8] This soul was charged with the management of the body and its functions; it could be "lost" without death immediately ensuing, but it was still necessary for normal existence.[9] At some time after birth, a second soul called the *hun* came into being. This oversaw the "higher" realm of the person's intellectual and spiritual life. The *hun* soul was also capable of leaving the body temporarily under certain conditions[10]; in later times, this was to become a standard interpretation of the act of dreaming.

Both *po* and *hun* quit the body at death, the *hun* to rise into the air and the *po* to linger by the corpse. Thus, Han dynasty funeral ritual (second century B.C.E.–second century C.E.) included a ritual called the "summons" (*fu*) to recall the *hun*-soul. Only after being formally summoned without success could the survivors of the deceased be assured that the person was really dead and that the funeral could proceed.[11] After the funeral, the ancestral spirits had to be maintained in appropriate style, with sacrifices that continued on a diminishing scale for five generations. Sacrifice was a feeding of the dead in a literal sense[12]: a spirit denied sacrifice, or other appropriate dignities, would be hungry, dissatisfied, and potentially active for evil in the world of the living. It was intended not merely to avoid harm but to secure blessings, hence Confucius's remark that sacrificing to a spirit not one's own was "flattery."[13] Access to the dead was access to power, and this may have been why the ritual texts limited the number of ancestral shrines officers were allowed to maintain and forbade them entirely to commoners.[14]

One problem with this theoretical system is the difficulty in reconciling the multi-part soul with conceptions of the afterlife. On the one hand, from early times there were separate provisions for the *hun* and the *po* in the next world, which indicates that both were assumed to take on an independent otherworldly existence.[15] On the other hand, ghost tales and religious stories deal with the actions of a single entity, whether it is labeled *hun*, *po*, or something else; there seems to be none in which more than one type of spirit from a single person carries his or her consciousness and personality.[16]

GOING TO ONE'S REWARD

> His soul will be imprisoned and his doings in life will be questioned. If his words in life are found to be inconsistent, he will be subject to further imprisonment and torture. His soul is surely going to suffer a great deal. But who is to blame?[17]

A fourth-century C.E. collection of Daoist stories tells how, some two centuries before, Du Xie, governor of Jiaozhou, had died of accidental poisoning. Fortunately for him, the Daoist master Dong Feng was in the area and succeeded in reviving him. Several days after his return, Du Xie gave this account of his experiences:

> When I died, it was suddenly as if I had entered a dream. I saw a dozen black-clothed men come and put me into a cart. We departed, and went into a great red gate, passing through it for me to be consigned to a prison. The prisons each had one door, and the door had only enough space to admit one person. They put me through one, and sealed it up from the exterior with earth, so that I could see no light from outside. Suddenly I heard men's voices outside, saying "Taiyi [Grand Unity, a deity] has sent a messenger to summon Du Xie!" I also heard them digging out the earth blocking up the door. After a while, I was pulled out, and I saw there three men on a horse-cart with a red canopy. The

> senior one entered with a tally, and shouted, "Xie, get on the cart!" They took me back, and when I reached the gate, I woke up.[18]

Note that Du Xie does not seem to have been guilty of any particular sins. This was no more than a prosaic variant on the various fates awaiting you when you died: even if you escaped torment, you might be kept locked away forever, under the thumb of an otherworldly bureaucracy far more fearsome than the mundane governments of the world of light. The pattern of summons, arrest, and imprisonment recurs throughout Chinese history: "They murmur that they see evil spirits coming for them, and say, 'I see this and that other spirit,' so that one attendant dare not stay alone in the room with them."[19] The Chinese word for hell is *di yu*, the Prisons of the Earth, where the guilty-by-definition dead serve out their sentences.

This infernal state has sometimes been assumed to be a Buddhist introduction to Chinese thought, which supplanted an earlier and vaguer concept of most of the dead going to a dim subterranean realm, the Yellow Springs, while the souls of the kings rose up to join the court of the Lord on High.[20] However, it is now clear that many of its most characteristic details predate Buddhism in China. A short tale from around 300 B.C.E., discovered only recently, gives the earliest known reference: after the suicide of a man named Tan, he is returned to life when a co-worker sues the officials in charge of the world of the dead, claiming that Tan's lifetime is not yet complete.[21] It would seem that even by that date, the next world had become essentially a duplicate of this one. As Arthur Wolf remarked,

> Judged in terms of its administrative arrangements, the Chinese imperial government looks impotent. Assessed in terms of its long-range impact on the people, it appears to have been one of the most potent governments ever known, for it created a religion in its own image.[22]

Here we see the disadvantage of an organic world-system: alive or dead, there was literally nowhere to hide. Around 600

B.C.E., a poet wrote, "In all under Heaven, there is none not the king's land; to the borders of the seas, there are none not the king's subjects."[23] Proud words already, but three centuries later the king's realm had grown until he claimed hegemony over all that lived or had ever lived, in the skies, on the earth, and in the infernal regions. By the middle of the Han, around the beginning of the common era, the lord of the dead was being addressed as if he were just another provincial governor. In one text he is even called the *grandson* of Heaven, underlining his position as the obedient and filial subordinate of the emperor of China, the Son of Heaven.[24]

One telltale sign of how contemporaries regarded their postmortem prospects is the lengths the living would go to in order to ensure that the dead never returned. Han funerals may have included a "recall," but any later appearance of a ghost, who would be in effect a prison escapee, was a highly inauspicious sign of cosmic irregularity. This is why, for instance, tomb texts from the first few centuries C.E. demand so insistently that the dead remain far from the living: "Promptly remove yourself three thousand leagues away! Should you not go away, the [. . .] of Southern Mountain will be ordered to come and devour you. Promptly, in accordance with the statutes and ordinances!"[25] The final phrase, taken directly from the phraseology of government decrees, is echoed throughout Chinese history; the commands of legitimate authority bind the dead as tightly as the living.

The impact of Buddhism, which began to seep into China sometime in the first century C.E., was as immense in the conceptualization of the afterlife as it was in other areas, though it did more to shape what was already there and less to introduce new ideas than previously thought. Its two most prominent contributions were 1) the idea of the *rebirth* of the soul, and 2) a thorough systemization and rationalization of the nether regions, so that they became predominantly a place where one's sins were paid for, with excruciating thoroughness.[26] The earliest sutras to be translated seem to have included some on avoiding untimely death, and the idea of karma caught Chinese imaginations easily.[27] However, it was almost totally misunderstood, especially during the first centuries, as evidenced most plainly by the debate in the sixth century C.E. at the Liang court on whether the soul survived the body at death. The destruction of the soul was argued by Fan Zhen, a Confucian who bitterly opposed Buddhism; the immortality of the soul was proclaimed by his Buddhist opponents, who were as yet unaware that they were arguing a totally heretical position judged by the standards of orthodox Buddhism.[28]

After its introduction the Buddhist tradition began its steady climb to the position it was to have until the end of the Imperial era: guardian to the passage through death. Under the combined influence of Buddhist thought and contributions from Daoism and popular religion, in the ninth or tenth century C.E. the next world finally assumed the shape it would have from that time to the present. This conception, the systemization of the underworld into the ten courts of hell, was actively propagated on all levels of society by art and storytelling. Painters, some of whom claimed to have visited the infernal regions and returned, began to specialize in hell scenes; for instance, the general Pei Mei asked one of these experts, Wu Dao, to paint figures of ghosts and spirits to aid his mother in the next world.[29] Home-cooked Buddhist apocrypha, such as the *Sutra of the Ten Kings*, aided in the ritual transformation by promising salvation to anyone whose family did the correct rituals to the ten kings, and damnation to those who did not, regardless of other merits.[30] A book written by a Daoist, Danchi, in the middle of the eleventh century, the *Yuli Chaozhuan*, gives a tour of hell, which became one of the most popular descriptions. It names all the judges, gives all the locations of the various hells, and includes extremely vivid sketches of the horrible fate lying in store for the various types of sinner, the latter specified in extremely minute detail. Thus, those who delay in delivering letters will be tormented under the supervision of the lord of the five senses in the fourth court of hell, and those who lie about their age on marriage contracts will face the rack, boiling cauldrons, sandstorms, ice, hunger, and much else in the second court under King Chujiang.[31] A peculiarly vindictive touch was the Pool of Blood, reserved for women, where they were punished for polluting the waters of the earth with the blood they shed in menstruation or childbirth, and from which the sole salvation lay in religious services by their sons or Buddhist priests after their deaths.[32]

There were more pleasant alternatives, though these could never be counted on. The summons could be to something more comfortable than a dark cell or torture chamber. An exceptionally just man, after death, might take up an exalted place in the next world. For instance, popular legend held it that Bao Zheng, a Song dynasty judge renowned for strictness and incorruptibility, occupied the seat of Yanluo Wang in hell, and that the judge of the Second Court had in life been Han Qinhu, Emperor Wen of Sui's prime minister, who was met at his death by a large escort of spirits to be conveyed to his new position as a king of hell.[33]

On a lower level, a badly mistreated person might enjoy revenge in ghostly form. As one woman in a story remarked at her execution:

> "Magistrate Tao knows all about this, but unjustly he still wants to kill me. If I don't become a ghost after I die, that'll be the end of it. But if I do become a ghost, I shall certainly file charges."[34]

She did, and returned in person to execute the errant official.

On a higher level, but one much more subject to the whims of chance, a deceased person, even a suicide, might succeed in entering the service of a deity or, even more rarely, might become a deity in his or her own right. The goddess of the privy, Lady Ding or Lady Purple, is one well-known example. In life she had been a concubine driven to hang herself in the privy by the cruelty of her master's wife; she later manifested spiritual power through mediums and became recognized as a divine protectress of women.[35]

PRISON BREAKS: PHILOSOPHY, ALCHEMY, ESCAPE, ENDURANCE

> Can being up in Heaven hold more joy than life among men? The only advantage is that nothing makes you grow

> old and die. Up in Heaven, there are lots of grand dignitaries, and truckling to them is even bitterer than it is among men.[36]

Even from the cursory sketch above, it is clear that, for many, life after death was nothing to look forward to. Whether the gray and dismal prison of the earliest conceptions or the more inventive purgatories of later religion, there seemed little there but much more of the same: torment by a corrupt administration ending in an oblivious rebirth and an uncertain future. Little wonder that part of the story of the afterlife in China is how the dead person might change his or her fate, mitigating the pains or perhaps even avoiding the experience altogether. Such escapes might be classified into three general forms: philosophical, technical, and religious.

The philosophical was the favorite of the Confucian literati and had a steady if not necessarily great influence on other sections of society. It relied on the implicit faith in the goodness of the natural order to deny that there was either anything to fear or anything to do the fearing. The soul, helped through the transition of state from living being to ancestor by the prescribed rituals, need only be served in the proper way and all would be well. Its multiple parts sank or scattered, and without much fuss reintegrated themselves into the cosmos. Provided human beings, the family of the deceased in particular, played their parts properly, everything would go smoothly. Nevertheless, to those too impatient to appreciate the philosophical subtlety of their position, it seemed that they were trying to have it both ways: an ancestral cult without ancestral spirits.[37]

With the rise, beginning around the tenth century, of the Neo-Confucian school, which mocked the popular idea of the afterlife as ridiculous and condemned Buddhism while borrowing at length from its more philosophical parts, there began a movement to return all aspects of family life to ancient standards, including funerals. One of the first direct attacks in this campaign was launched by Zhu Xi, the most important single figure in the Confucian revival. When serving in Zhangzhou, Fujian, in

1190 he demanded that all funerals hew to the Confucian line on pain of punishment for violators.[38] Even so, the burial that excluded Buddhist or Daoist participation and stuck strictly to the economy advocated by the Master remained exceptional. However much the idea of reincarnation offended literati sensibilities, they had nothing very comforting to put in the place of the Buddhist vision.[39]

A second approach to evading postmortem pains might be called the technical one. In the chaotic period of the later Warring States and the early Han, and again and far stronger in the later part of the Han and the four centuries of division that followed, the quest for personal autonomy took the guise of an "afterlife" consisting of an eternal extension of *this* life. One way was the adjustment of the diet to eliminate all gross and earthly matter from the body, to allow the adept literally to float up to Heaven.[40] Drugs that would eternally preserve the bodily frame were an easier way to the same goal; curiously enough, many of the compounds tried, preparations of arsenic and mercury, did have preservative powers, albeit only on corpses. At any rate, by mid-Han a number of miracle stories had begun to circulate, crediting otherwise quite ordinary people with the ability to transcend the world. One such was Tang Gongfang, a petty official at the end of Former Han in the provincial administration of Hanzhong. He had met a Daoist "True Man" and become his disciple, winning his favor; the True Man had given him enough of the drug of immortality that in 7 C.E. he was supposed to have risen up to Heaven, taking with him not only his family and his livestock, but even his house.[41]

Another possibility was to escape death in a paradise on earth, usually conceived of as a place just beyond the horizon where divine beings lived. One of the earlier forms of this was the island paradise just beyond the horizons in the Eastern Sea, Penglai, where the "drug of eternal life" was to be had for the taking. A parallel idea set in the opposite quarter was the realm of the Queen Mother of the West on Mount Kunlun, which had been in contact with the Central States during the time of the ancient sages. A steady increase in geographical knowledge later acted as a check on enthusiasms of this sort, but the lack of a true "other world"—the organic unity of the universe—led to the realm of the dead being placed at a definite point on earth. Thus, the residence of dead souls was seen as being under Mount Tai at the base of the Shandong Peninsula. Some Daoists considered the entrance to be in Fengtu in Sichuan,[42] and others located the basement of the next world, the dwelling place of the unperfected dead, in the Citadel of Night (Yecheng), located far to the north of China. In popular literature the idea lingered on. Thus in the *Record of the Three-Treasures Eunuch Going Down to the West*, written around 1600, the famous early Ming admiral, Zheng He, who was a Muslim, keeps on sailing west after arriving at Mecca until he touches land in the realm of the dead.[43] However, by that time these distant lands had all been brought under some sort of official structure, and the freedom of the early transcendents had been eliminated. Even as early as Maoshan Daoism (fourth century C.E.), the Cave-Heavens of Mount Luofeng in the far north had become the seat of an otherworldly bureaucracy, albeit one not subordinate to the temporal Son of Heaven.[44]

Both alchemy and flight beyond society were dreams restricted almost entirely to the upper classes; the common people by and large accepted the bureaucratization of the nether world and tried their best to work within it, just as for the most part they endured the misbehavior of their earthly rulers.[45] The rituals of popular religion are thus designed to guide the soul of the dying person through the transition from life to death,[46] manipulating and controlling spirits and ghosts by such means as the carefully graded use of food offerings, which affirm relationship, and spirit money, which establishes social distance. As with more intellectual schemes, the paramount value is order, and the measures taken are designed to re-create or enhance order. For instance, one ritual is designed to deal with children attacked by night terrors, attributed to the resentment of their parents in a past life who have been slower to attain rebirth than their former child.[47] Other arrangements are aimed toward the integration of souls that have no certain place in the family scheme; for instance, young children who die with no one to sacrifice to them are either considered a manifestation of nonhuman demons or their worship ends up deferred one or two generations, until supernatural manifestations make it clear to their juniors that they deserve sacrifice. Unmarried women, who have not succeeded in joining themselves to a husband's family as is proper, are settled by arranging marriages between their ghosts and a living man (which ensures them of at least one adopted child to venerate them)[48] or by putting their souls into the charge of a spirit medium.

There remain the truly unknown ghosts: strangers or those without family. Popular religion deals with them as well, since harmony requires ideally the reintegration of every person, dead or alive, stranger or relative, enemy or friend. The *pudu* or "universal salvation" ritual in the seventh lunar month is thus designed to empty the infernal regions, ending the punishment of their residents and allowing them to escape.[49] On the fifteenth day of that month every household is supposed to make offerings, presented outside the house and facing away from it, to anonymous ghosts. This is not a veneration but a precaution, for even the lowest and least regarded of supernatural creatures must receive their due for the last impediment to the smooth functioning of Heaven and Earth to be removed.[50]

THE AFTERLIFE IN "AFTER-TIMES"

> Since worldly people have adopted modern behavior patterns, the netherworld has added many new halls of punishment.[51]

Traditional ideas of the afterlife are alive and well in Chinese culture, especially in those places where that culture has been allowed to develop without official disturbance. Even in Mainland China the country people, who form the absolute majority of China's population, never forgot their old gods and, just as in Taiwan, increasing prosperity will inevitably bring the deities larger temples and more elaborate devotions. Quite apart from the fact that many of the most popular of the gods began as human beings, the traditional complex of ideas concerning the afterlife is an essential part of this world view, and the extreme flexibility of Chinese popular religion allows it to treat different traditions as complementary, not contradictory.[52] Nevertheless, both in China and overseas, the insidious pressures of the modern world may be beginning to erode the concrete force that terror of the ten kings might once have wielded.[53] Many believers are now motivated more by pity for lost ghosts than by fear of their power to do evil, or at least this is what they tell foreign ethnologists.[54]

Does this mean that belief in the ghosts and their shadowy world might eventually disappear? Perhaps not. One should never underestimate the vitality of popular belief. Moreover, the "Confucian" world view that has been promoted as a superior replacement for "superstition" has a highly developed talent for subsuming what it considers the vulgar rites to common gods, infusing them with a this-worldly significance that eclipses their actuality and makes rituals to them a fitting part of the Way of Man. Ritual has a meaning that goes beyond its contents and apparatus to encapsulate the attitudes it encourages, evokes, and inspires in others. Some of the worshipers who burn paper money to ancestors in present-day Taiwan may not be convinced that the spirits actually seize upon these tokens in the next world and hurry off to pay their infernal debts. They might not believe in spirits at all, but they believe in respect for the social order, which extends through time and thus transcends death, and they believe that the ceremonial sacrifice of a symbol of wealth can symbolize the enduring value of the family and the social order. The spirits may fade, but the spirit will remain.

Notes

[1] Quoted in Julian F. Pas, "*Journey to Hell*: A New Report of Shamanistic Travel to the Courts of Hell," *Journal of Chinese Religions* 17 (Fall 1989), p. 59, from the "morality text" (*shanshu*) *Journey to Hell*,

which was revealed via spirit writing in Taiwan in 1978. By 1989 five million copies of this two-hundred-page book had been distributed.

[2] Chinese conceptions of the afterlife can be almost absurdly close to the way things are in the world of light. One late source even asserts that ghosts can die and become "ghost ghosts," and that ghost ghosts frighten ghosts in the same way that ghosts frighten men (Anthony Yü, "'Rest, Rest, Perturbed Spirit!' Ghosts in Traditional Chinese Prose Fiction," *Harvard Journal of Asiatic Studies* 47/2 [1987], p. 432, n.58). The conservatism of the next world is evident from many details; for instance, Wolf reports that the accepted gift to require answered prayers in one temple that houses the spirits of unmarried girls is a pair of children's shoes, "because women in the im [Yin; dark] world still have bound feet" (Arthur P. Wolf, "Gods, Ghosts, and Ancestors," in *Religion and Ritual in Chinese Society*, ed. Arthur P. Wolf [Stanford: Stanford University Press, 1974], p. 150).

[3] *Analects* XI/12, my own translation, which stresses the implications of the negative and the interrogative used by Confucius—*wei*, "not yet, never yet, never" (negation as a continuing state) and *yan*, "how, where, from what, on what basis."

[4] The majority of Chinese gods began as living persons. Both as gods and as dead persons, they retain individual preferences and idiosyncracies (cf. Stevan Harrell, "The Concept of Soul in Chinese Folk Religion," *Journal of Asian Studies* 38/3 [May 1979], p. 519).

[5] For an example of Neo-Confucian attacks on Buddhism, including but not limited to its attitude toward life, see the long polemic quoted in Joseph Needham, *Science and Civilisation in China*, Volume 2: *History of Scientific Thought* (Cambridge: Cambridge University Press, 1956), pp. 413-16, translated from the *Beiqi Ziyi* of Chen Shun (ca. 1200 C.E.).

[6] This is why there is no glorification of war in Chinese philosophy. Even the Legalist school, which one would expect to extol warfare for its role in expanding and exalting state power, accepts that it is an ugly business and assumes that people will only go to battle if they are given no other choice.

[7] Cf. Yü Ying-shih, "Life and Immortality in the Mind of Han China," *Harvard Journal of Asiatic Studies* 25 (1964-65), pp. 81-87.

[8] The *locus classicus* for this theory is the *Zuo* tradition (*Zuozhuan*), a historical text written around 300 B.C.E. based on earlier materials, in an entry dated to the seventh year of Duke Zhao, or 534 B.C.E. (James Legge, trans., *The Chinese Classics*, Volume 5: *The Ch'un Ts'ew with*

the Tso Chuen [Taipei: Wenshezhe chubanshe repr., 1972], p. 618). The *po* and *hun* were multiplied by later theorists, who also added a "fetus-spirit" that came into existence at the moment of conception and lasted until a few months after birth at most. It resides around the house, its location changing daily, and if it is inadvertently harmed the unborn child may be deformed or diseased (cf. Harrell, pp. 523-24).

[9] Yü Ying-shih, "'O Soul, Come Back!' A Study in Changing Conceptions of the Soul and Afterlife in Han China," *Harvard Journal of Asiatic Studies* 47/2 (1987), pp. 370-71.

[10] Harrell remarks, "The ling-hun does not exactly give life to the body: the body can exist, at least temporarily, without any ling-hun. What a body without a ling-hun is missing is not life but humanity, defined in terms of the culturally accepted and assumed forms of appropriate behavior in a Chinese context" (p. 527).

[11] Yü Ying-shih, "Oh Soul, Come Back!" pp. 365-69.

[12] Duke Xuan 4th year, 604 B.C.E., records the fear of a nobleman in peril that his family's spirits will be starved if their descendants are wiped out (Legge, p. 297).

[13] *Analects* II/24.

[14] Cf. "The Royal Regulations" ("Wang Zhi"), a chapter in the *Record of Rituals* (James Legge, trans., *Li Chi: Book of Rites*, ed. Ch'u Chai and Winberg Chai [New York: University Books, 1967], vol. 1, p. 223).

[15] Yü Ying-shih, "Oh Soul, Come Back!" pp. 392-93.

[16] Harrell reviews the arguments for the various numbers of souls and concludes that "when non-specialists talk in any context about the ling-hun as an entity with attributes, whether it be the fetus-spirit before birth, something which has gone from the body and so caused mental illness, or what has become a shen [divinity] or kuei [ghost], they usually speak of a single entity. . . . I think that the ling-hun [soul] in the tablet, the ling-hun in the grave, and the ling-hun in the yin world are not so much separate 'souls' as separate contexts. When rural Taiwanese perform ancestral sacrifices at home, they naturally think of the ling-hun in the tablet; when they take offerings to the cemetery, they think of it in the grave; and when they go on shamanistic trips, they think of it in the yin world. Because the contexts are separate, there is little conflict and little need for abstract reasoning about a nonexistent problem" (pp. 522-23).

This popular consensus may be based on a cosmological principle, shared by elite and popular culture, that things of the same type stimulate each other. Such stimulus does not require a direct physical connection, though it was often conceived of in mechanistic terms (one favorite classical example was a tuned string vibrating when another string tuned to the same note was plucked). Since the grave, the ancestral tablet, and the soul or souls are all eminently "of the same kind," it would be entirely reasonable to believe in them being joined by a "wireless network" of mutual stimulus and response, especially since the *hun*-soul, being composed of exceptionally subtle material, would be correspondingly sensitive.

[17] From the Daoist *Canon of Great Peace*, second–fifth centuries C.E., quoted in Yü Ying-shih, "O Soul, Come Back!" p. 390.

[18] Ge Hong (died ca. 360 C.E.), *Biographies of Divine Transcendents* (*Shenxian zhuan*), ed. Longwei bishu, 6/10a-b. The authenticity of this text has been challenged, but most if not all of it seems to go back to the fourth century C.E.

[19] R. L. McNabb, *The Women of the Middle Kingdom* (New York: Young People's Missionary Movement, 1907), pp. 139-40.

[20] This was the picture in the north; southern ideas were very different, seeing deadly threats to the wandering soul in all four directions and above and below as well (cf. the description in Laurence G. Thompson, "On the Prehistory of Hell in China," *Journal of Chinese Religions* 17 [Fall 1989], pp. 28-33). The heavens remain the destination of the dead in some later tales, but usually the journey there is to pay court to a deity, not for permanent residence (Robert F. Campany, "Return-From-Death Narratives in Early Medieval China," *Journal of Chinese Religions* 18 [Fall 1990], pp. 103-6).

[21] See Donald Harper's bibliographic review of material on Warring States religion, *Journal of Asian Studies* 54/1 (February 1995), p. 158.

[22] Wolf, p. 145.

[23] *Canon of Poetry* #240, "Beishan."

[24] Cf. Yü Ying-shih, "O Soul, Come Back!" pp. 388-90, and the extract from the *Accounts of Mirabelia* (*Bowu zhi*) by Zhang Hua (232-300 C.E.), translated in Campany, p. 107.

[25] Anna Seidel, "*Post-Mortem* Immortality, or the Taoist Resurrection of the Body," in *Gilgul: Essays on Transformation, Revolution, and Permanence in the History of Religions*, ed. S. Shaked, D. Shulman, G. G. Stroumsa (Leiden: E. J. Brill, 1987), p. 228.

[26] Thompson notes that the first-century B.C.E. skeptic Wang Chong, who ridicules popular concepts of spirits at every turn, never mentions posthumous judgment or punishment. The first clear appearance of

this theme is more than a century later, in Daoist popular religious movements; and even then it is the living who are punished for their own sins or those of their ancestors, by having sickness inflicted on them by the authorities of the nether regions (pp. 36-38).

[27] Stephen F. Teiser, "'Having Once Died and Returned to Life': Representations of Hell in Medieval China," *Harvard Journal of Asiatic Studies* 48/2 (1988), p. 460.

[28] On this debate see, among others, Walter Libenthal, "The Immortality of the Soul in Chinese Thought," *Monumenta Nipponica* 8:1-2 (January 1952), pp. 327-97; Etienne Balazs, "The First Chinese Materialist," in Etienne Balazs, *Chinese Civilization and Bureaucracy*, ed. Arthur Wright (New Haven: Yale University Press, 1964), pp. 255-76; and Whalen Lai, "Beyond the Debate on 'The Immortality of the Soul': Recovering an Essay by Shen Yueh," *Journal of Oriental Studies* (Hong Kong) 19/2 (1981), pp. 138-57.

[29] Teiser, pp. 439-43.

[30] Ibid., pp. 451-52.

[31] Anne Swann Goodrich, *Chinese Hells: The Peking Temple of Eighteen Hells and Chinese Conceptions of Hell* (St. Augustin: Monumenta Serica, 1971), pp. 74-75.

[32] Ibid., pp. 55-56, 65.

[33] Ibid., pp. 82–85.

[34] Anthony Yü, pp. 417-19.

[35] Ibid., p. 420.

[36] *Biographies of Divine Transcendents* (*Shenxian zhuan*), Longwei bishu edition, 2/1b.

[37] As Mozi (fourth century B.C.E.), the earliest and one of the harshest critics of Confucius is supposed to have put it, "When a parent dies, the Confucians lay out the corpse for a long time before dressing it for burial while they climb up onto the roof, peer down the well, poke in the ratholes, and search in the washbasins, looking for the dead man. If they suppose that they will really find the dead man there, then they must be stupid indeed, while if they know that he is not there but still search for him, then they are guilty of the greatest hypocrisy" (Burton Watson, trans., *Mo Tzu: Basic Writings* [New York: Columbia University Press, 1963], p. 125).

[38] Evelyn S. Rawski, "A Historian's Approach to Chinese Death Ritual," in *Death Ritual in Late Imperial and Modern China*, ed. James L. Watson and Evelyn S. Rawski (Berkeley: University of California Press, 1988), p. 30.

[39] One thing that made Confucians uneasy about the Buddhist scheme was the possibility that one's parents might be reincarnated as one's junior or even an animal. For a general account of the movement to return to ancient funeral rituals, see Timothy Brook, "Funerary Ritual and the Building of Lineages in Late Imperial China," *Harvard Journal of Asiatic Studies* 49/2 (1989), pp. 465-99.

[40] An early example of this method is the fourth-century B.C.E. story about the immortal of Guyi Mountain, who had foresworn a diet of grain to exist on wind and dew, and who had in consequence gained the power to prevent plague and ensure the ripening of the crops (see A. C. Graham, *Chuang-tzu: The Inner Chapters* [London: George Allen and Unwin, 1981], p. 46). Zhuangzi's own "rhapsodic" acceptance of death is often cited, but it is so exceptional that relating it at length would risk misleading the reader in a general survey such as this. Those interested may consult the introduction in Graham's translation (pp. 23-24) and the relevant sections of the text.

[41] See Yü, "Life and Immortality," p. 107. For a thorough treatment of Chinese alchemy, including the drugs of immortality, see Joseph Needham, *Science and Civilisation in China*, Volume 5:2: *Chemistry and Chemical Technology*, Part II: *Spagyrical Discovery and Invention: Magisteries of Gold and Immortality* (Cambridge: Cambridge University Press, 1974).

[42] Duane Pang, "The *P'u-tu* Ritual: A Celebration of the Chinese Community of Honolulu," in *Buddhist and Taoist Studies I*, ed. Michael Saso and David W. Chappell (University Press of Hawaii, 1977), pp. 95-122, especially p. 100.

[43] Goodrich, pp. 88–96; J. J. L. Duyvendak, "A Chinese 'Divina Commedia,'" *T'oung Pao* 41 (1952), pp. 255-316.

[44] See the description in Thompson, pp. 38-41.

[45] Just as in the political area, the tolerance of the commoners for religious oppression was not unlimited. The popular equivalents to alchemy or otherworldly flight were the salvationist cults, which preached access to a paradise seen in popular Buddhist terms, such as the White Lotus sects of late Imperial China. These aimed at enabling their believers, as one said, to "ascend directly to Heaven, meet together with the Eternal Mother, and never again return to this world" (Daniel Overmyer, *Folk Buddhist Religion* [Cambridge: Harvard University Press, 1976], p. 191). Another said that anyone with one of the "passports" provided by their teachers and burned at death "would be met and led through hell by a god and would not have to suffer hell's

bitterness" (Susan Naquin, "Funerals in North China: Uniformity and Variation," in Watson and Rawski, p. 51).

[46] The exact details of these techniques vary in different regions of China, but all concur in assuming that death is a crisis point that holds great potential for creating cosmic disorder, and every action must thus be carefully choreographed. We have mentioned Naquin's article on North China funerals above (see note 45); an interesting essay on attitudes in south China is James L. Watson, "Of Flesh and Bones: The Management of Death Pollution in Cantonese Society," in *Death and the Regeneration of Life*, ed. Jonathan Parry and Maurice Bloch (Cambridge: Cambridge University Press, 1982), pp. 155-86.

[47] John L. McCreery, "Why Don't We See Some Real Money Here?—Offerings in Chinese Religion," *Journal of Chinese Religion* 18 (Fall 1990), pp. 1-24.

[48] Stevan Harrell, "Men, Women, and Ghosts in Taiwanese Folk Religion," *Gender and Religion: On the Complexity of Symbols*, ed. Caroline Walker Bynum, Stevan Harrell, Paula Richman (Boston: Beacon Press, 1986), pp. 98-100.

[49] Pang.

[50] Harrell "Men, Women, and Ghosts," pp. 104-6.

[51] Quoted in Pas, p. 58.

[52] This has had an interesting reflection in the nether world, if we can trust the account in *Journey to Hell*: a new antechamber has been added to the halls of punishment, with the motto "All Teachings Return To Unity" inscribed over its gate, a place for the departed spirits of missionaries who intolerantly denigrate other sects to contemplate the errors of their ways without actually having to endure the torments of the hells (Pas, pp. 59-60).

[53] Jeffrey Meyer summarizes their view of religion thusly: "Much of it is superstition and ought to be discarded. But some religions do preserve important values, especially in upholding morality and public order. However, one who follows Confucius (though this view is never directly stated) has all these values already and has no need for the religious trappings which go with them" ("The Image of Religion in Taiwan Textbooks," *Journal of Chinese Religions* 15 [Fall 1987], p. 50).

[54] Robert P. Weller, "Bandits, Beggars, and Ghosts: The Failure of State Control over Religious Interpretation in Taiwan," *American Ethnologist* 12/1 (February 1985), p. 54.

About the Authors

Harold Coward is Professor of History and Director of the Centre for Studies in Religion and Society at the University of Victoria. His main fields are comparative religion; psychology of religion; and environmental ethics. He serves as an Executive Member of the Board, Canadian Global Change Program. His wide variety of publications include *Ethics and Climate Change* (with Thomas Hurka) (1993) and *Pluralism: Challenge to World Religions* (1985).

Eliezer Segal is Associate Professor in the Department of Religious Studies at the University of Calgary. He received the Ph.D. in Talmud from the Hebrew University of Jerusalem in 1982. He is the author of *Case Citation in the Babylonian Talmud* (1990), *The Babylonian Esther Midrash: A Critical Commentary* (three volumes, 1994) and various chapters and articles dealing with aspects of Rabbinic literature, Jewish law, and comparative biblical exegesis.

Terence Penelhum is Professor Emeritus of Religious Studies at the University of Calgary, where he was formerly Professor of Philosophy, Dean of Arts and Science, and a Director of the Institute for the Humanities. He is a graduate of Edinburgh and Oxford. His books include *Survival and Disembodied Existence* (1970), *God and Skepticism* (1983), and *Reason and Religious Faith* (1995). He was awarded the Canada Council Molson Prize in the Humanities in 1988.

Hanna Kassis is Professor of Near Eastern and Islamic Studies in the Department of Classical, Near Eastern, and Religious Studies at the University of British Columbia. He received his undergraduate and part of his graduate training at the American University of Beirut. He obtained the Ph.D. in Near Eastern Languages and Civilization from Harvard University in 1965. Although his initial training was in the Ancient Near East, his research interests shifted to Islamic studies, where he applies the methodology he acquired for his earlier studies. His interest focuses on Muslim Spain and on Muslim-Christian relations there. In addition to his *Concordance of the Qur'an* (Berkeley, 1983) and a Spanish equivalent, *Las Concordancias del Corán* (Madrid, 1987), his many articles focus on the revival of orthodoxy among Muslims and the Christian response to this revival.

Anantanand Rambachan is Professor of Religion at Saint Olaf College in Northfield, Minnesota, U.S.A. He is the author of several books including *The Limits of Sculpture: Vivekananda's Reinterpretation of the Authority of the Vedas*, and *Accomplishing the Accomplished: The Vedas as a Source of Valid Knowledge in Sankara*. A series of twenty-one lectures by Rambachan has been transmitted around the world by the British Broadcasting Corporation. He is a recipient of Trinidad's second-highest national honor, the Chaconia Gold Medal, for public service.

Eva K. Neumaier-Dargyay is Professor of Buddhist Religion and Literature in the Division of Comparative Studies in Literature, Film, and Religion at the University of Alberta, Edmonton. She received her Dr.Phil. and Dr.Phil.Habil. in Indian and Tibetan Studies from the Ludwig-Maximilians University, Munich, Germany, in 1966 and 1976 respectively. Her work is in the area of Tibetan religion and literature. Her latest book is *The Sovereign All-Creating Mind, the Motherly Buddha* (1992).

Gary Arbuckle is a Social Sciences and Humanities Research Fellow with the Department of Asian Studies, University of British Columbia. He received the Ph.D. from UBC in 1991. His chief field of research is the Confucian *Annals* traditions in Warring

States and Han China, and the early development of Chinese cosmology, concerning which he has published a number of articles, with a book in preparation on the Former Han Confucian thinker Dong Zhongshu, as well as an annotated translation of the *Chunqiu fanlu* (*Luxuriant Dew of the Annals*).

Index

Other Titles in the Faith Meets Faith Series

Toward a Universal Theology of Religion, Leonard Swidler, Editor
The Myth of Christian Uniqueness, John Hick and Paul F. Knitter, Editors
An Asian Theology of Liberation, Aloysius Pieris, S.J.
The Dialogical Imperative, David Lochhead
Love Meets Wisdom, Aloysius Pieris, S.J.
Many Paths, Eugene Hillman, C.S.Sp.
The Silence of God, Raimundo Panikkar
The Challenge of the Scriptures, Groupe de Recherches Islamo-Chrétien
The Meaning of Christ, John P. Keenan
Hindu-Christian Dialogue, Harold Coward, Editor
The Emptying God, John B. Cobb, Jr., and Christopher Ives, Editors
Christianity Through Non-Christian Eyes, Paul J. Griffiths, Editor
Christian Uniqueness Reconsidered, Gavin D'Costa, Editor
Women Speaking, Women Listening, Maura O'Neill
Bursting the Bonds?, Leonard Swidler, Lewis John Eron, Gerard Sloyan, and Lester Dean, Editors
One Christ—Many Religions, Stanley J. Samartha
The New Universalism, David J. Krieger
Jesus Christ at the Encounter of World Religions, Jacques Dupuis, S.J.
After Patriarchy, Paula M. Cooey, William R. Eakin, and Jay B. McDaniel, Editors
An Apology for Apologetics, Paul J. Griffiths
World Religions and Human Liberation, Dan Cohn-Sherbok, Editor
Uniqueness, Gabriel Moran
Leave the Temple, Felix Wilfred, Editor

The Buddha and the Christ, Leo D. Lefebure
The Divine Matrix, Joseph A. Bracken, S.J.
The Gospel of Mark: A Mahāyāna Reading, John P. Keenan
Revelation, History and the Dialogue of Religions, David A. Carpenter
Salvations, S. Mark Heim
The Intercultural Challenge of Raimon Panikkar, Joseph Prabhu, Editor
Fire and Water: Women, Society, and Spirituality in Buddhism and Christianity, Aloysius Pieris, S.J.